Praise for

how to stop breaking your own heart

'I love The Good Quote, so it's no surprise I love this book. Meggan's unique voice teaches us to accept ourselves as we are and to cultivate self-love.'

Steven Bartlett, #1 *Sunday Times* best-selling author and host of *The Diary of a CEO* podcast

'Meggan's words have the power to make you feel seen, understood, and less alone. This book is the reminder you need that you are worthy of self-love and acceptance.'

Jay Shetty, #1 *New York Times* best-selling author of *Think Like a Monk* and host of the *On Purpose* podcast

'I've been a huge fan of Meggan's writing from the very first time I read and felt her work. I can't wait for the release of her debut book – the world needs her work now more than ever!'

Hussain Manawer, *Sunday Times* best-selling author of *Life Is Sad and Beautiful*

'The book you need to learn to love yourself again, ensuring you never forget your worth.'

Yung Pueblo, #1 *New York Times* best-selling author

'Meggan's beautiful, heart-opening book is simultaneously raw, emotional, and wonderfully uplifting.'
Gabby Bernstein, #1 *New York Times* best-selling author

'This book is the reminder that everything you want is already on its way to you.'
Lewis Howes, *New York Times* best-selling author and host of *The School of Greatness* podcast

'Meggan's words soothe the broken parts of us and show us how to nurture our hearts through life's ups and downs.'
Najwa Zebian, best-selling author of *Welcome Home*

'Your time is diamonds. Meggan shares her expertise on the art of setting boundaries while also providing valuable insights on how to manage pushback from those around us. Her advice is an essential tool for anyone looking to protect their time and establish healthy boundaries.'
Eve Rodsky, *New York Times* best-selling author of *Fair Play*

how to
stop
breaking
your own
heart

how to stop breaking your own heart

MEGGAN ROXANNE

HAY HOUSE

Carlsbad, California • New York City
London • Sydney • New Delhi

Published in the United Kingdom by:
Hay House UK Ltd, The Sixth Floor, Watson House, 54 Baker Street
London W1U 7BU
Tel: +44 (0)20 3927 7290; www.hayhouse.co.uk

Published in the United States of America by:
Hay House LLC, PO Box 5100, Carlsbad, CA 92018-5100
Tel: (1) 760 431 7695 or (800) 654 5126; www.hayhouse.com

Published in Australia by:
Hay House Australia Publishing Pty Ltd, 18/36 Ralph St, Alexandria NSW 2015
Tel: (61) 2 9669 4299; www.hayhouse.com.au

Published in India by:
Hay House Publishers (India) Pvt Ltd, Muskaan Complex, Plot No.3, B-2,
Vasant Kunj, New Delhi 110 070
Tel: (91) 11 4176 1620; www.hayhouse.co.in

Text © Meggan Roxanne, 2024

The moral rights of the author have been asserted.

The information given in this book should not be treated as a substitute for professional
medical advice; always consult a medical practitioner. Any use of information in this book is
at the reader's discretion and risk. Neither the author
nor the publisher can be held responsible for any loss, claim or damage arising
out of the use, or misuse, of the suggestions made, the failure to take medical
advice or for any material on third-party websites.

A catalogue record for this book is available from the British Library.

Tradepaper ISBN: 978-1-4019-7584-5
E-book ISBN: 978-1-83782-086-3
Audiobook ISBN: 978-1-83782-085-6

10 9 8 7 6 5 4 3 2 1

Printed in the United States of America

This product uses responsibly sourced papers and/or recycled materials. For more
information, see www.hayhouse.com.

SUSTAINABLE FORESTRY INITIATIVE Certified Chain of Custody
Promoting Sustainable Forestry
www.forests.org
SFI-01268
SFI label applies to the text stock

I dedicate this book to my late mother,

Janette Carol Harewood – my epitome of love.

You were phenomenal. Rest peacefully, my love.

Infinite, everlasting love.

Meggie.

xxxxxxxxxxxxxxxxxxxxxxxxxxxxxxxXxxx*

It is well – give thanks.

---

*   When my mum and I wrote cards to each other, we'd add an extra 'x' every year. The 32nd 'x' is in bold because that's the age I was when my mum passed away.

Contents

2

how we start to heal our hearts

3

how we nurture and protect our hearts

Introduction

Healing has a gentle way of surprising us when we least expect it.

For me, healing arrived during one of my daily morning walks in my local park, one crisp autumn morning. The farther I walked into the forest, the quieter it became. As my thoughts began to settle, the natural sounds around me forced me to stop and embrace my surroundings. In that moment of solitude, I came to terms with how peaceful my life had become. I felt overwhelmed with appreciation for finally arriving at a place in my life where I could acknowledge the progress I'd made over the years. I'd manifested achieving that level of peace, and there I was, right in the middle of it. It was a moment of deep gratitude, a chance to acknowledge the stillness and beauty that my life still had to offer.

When I launched The Good Quote on Instagram back in 2014, my mission was clear: to build an online sanctuary where people could find a stream of meaningful, empowering words that truly resonated. During that period I was navigating my own battle with depression, and I really felt the absence of a supportive online community. I couldn't find any spaces or forums that provided me with much meaningful solace. So, I cultivated my own. I didn't expect the response to have such a far-reaching impact. The content I curated crossed borders and cultures and touched millions of lives on a global scale.

I teamed up with a group of emerging writers and content creators who generously contributed their words daily. The response was overwhelming. Our audience numbers skyrocketed, celebrities became frequent visitors, and we even sparked a global trend where people began replacing their profile pictures with quotes to better express their emotions. The impact was beyond anything I'd anticipated. I realized I'd created a space that genuinely acknowledged and validated people's feelings, and the significance of that truly hit home.

I'll never forget the day we received a message from a mother who had recently lost her daughter to suicide. She expressed her gratitude for our community after finding a folder labeled 'Hope' on her daughter's laptop, filled with uplifting content, including many quotes from our platform. That moment deeply affected me and served as a reminder of how a few compassionate words can be a beacon of light in someone's darkest hours.

When I started The Good Quote, I wasn't trying to cater to a specific demographic. My goal was to foster a community that united people through the emotional experiences we all have but rarely talk about. The project came from a place of intuition, and its success was a clear sign that I had touched on something that resonated with a wider audience.

It's affirming to see that beneath the many layers that differentiate us, whether it's age, cultural background, or personal beliefs, we all share an emotional common ground. We all go through ups and downs, and moments of joy, as well as pain. It's all connected and it's beautiful.

I want this book to contain the same essence as The Good Quote; I want to weave together these universal experiences to help guide us through the complexities of life. I hope there's at least one story, if not more, that resonates with you so you can feel seen, understood, and less alone. I hope it sparks many *Ahh, I know exactly where you're coming from* moments – but more than anything, I hope this book serves as a gentle reminder, affirming that whatever challenges you're facing, you possess the resilience and capability to rise above them. Because the truth is, we all have the capacity to tackle any challenge that comes our way.

I've been through the trenches of trauma, and I'm still here. I've gone through some intense experiences in my life and broken my own heart many times over, through successes and setbacks, joy and despair, love and loss, self-discovery and self-doubt. But going through all these ups and downs has drawn something profound out of me. Through every twist and turn of my journey, I've learned that being open and vulnerable is the bridge to moving forward.

Trust me, vulnerability is a strength that is often underestimated. When I choose to be vulnerable by showing empathy and patience, I'm not just avoiding conflict; I'm creating a space where understanding can thrive. For example, say someone close to me is going through a turbulent period in their life and it's resulted in their making harmful decisions that affect them emotionally. By being vulnerable and resonating with them through sharing a personal story, I'm able to reassure them they're not alone, and that they can also overcome their difficult circumstance. By allowing ourselves to be vulnerable, we open ourselves up to this incredible power and strength.

Even though writing this book and sharing my deepest feelings with you ranks as one of the most daunting and challenging experiences of my life, I'm fully aware that making myself vulnerable in this way is also one of the most empowering things I could possibly do. I'm not going to pretend that I have it all figured out either – because I don't. There are moments when I'm still caught in a loop of detrimental habits. Take procrastination, for instance. It becomes my default escape when life gets too heavy. Or else, I'll convince myself that everyone else except me has their life sorted out perfectly. This pushes me to set impossible standards for myself, resulting in my being overwhelmed and stressed. In these moments, I often sit and ask myself: *How on earth can I teach others to stop breaking their own hearts when I'm still learning myself?*

I make mistakes, and self-doubt still shows up occasionally – I'm only human. But what I've come to understand is that healing is a never-ending journey. It requires the daily effort of replacing harmful coping mechanisms with healthier habits and facing the fears that come with making positive changes. The past may have its share of pain, but that doesn't mean we can't build meaningful lives moving forward.

The process of writing this book wasn't easy. The only thing that fueled my persistence and kept me going was envisioning a future moment where I could be on a train during the rush-hour commute, sitting across from someone who's completely absorbed in the very pages you're reading now. The thought of that future reader – *you* – filled me with so much joy, nervousness, and pure excitement.

My mum was a devoted reader; in fact, my favorite pastime was snuggling in bed as she read a chapter out loud. She had this incredible ability to lose herself in a good book, and her laughter would fill the room as she delved deeper into discovering a new author's story. Through her, I learned the transformative power of books. They can elevate your mood, change your life, and grant you access to someone else's experience, offering you a fresh perspective on the world.

So, I genuinely hope this book feels like a warm hug from me to you. I hope it serves as a reminder that every challenge, every obstacle, every heartache you're going through has a purpose.

Even if you've strayed miles away from where you're meant to be, just remember that you always have the power and the capability to return home to yourself.

It's time for you to stop breaking your own heart. So, let's get to the root of why we do this to ourselves, outline the first steps toward healing, and finally, let's work on building a life where self-care and the protection of our hearts are non-negotiable. I hope these pages serve as a reminder that everything you're going through in life has a purpose. This book is for you, a tool to accompany you on your journey and to welcome you back – with open arms – to who you really are.

1 how we break our own hearts

By choosing to pick up this book, you've taken an amazing step toward acknowledging that something in your life isn't functioning as you wish – there's something within that feels unresolved. Perhaps you resonated with the cover and felt the synergy between the title and the intentions that you're setting as you continue to dedicate yourself to healing.

It's a conscious decision to embark on a journey of self-improvement and emotional healing. It's also an incredible act of courage. However, before we can start the process of repairing and protecting our hearts, we must understand how and why we might end up breaking them. Maybe you feel unsure of how you arrived at this point, or maybe you've faced experiences that have severely altered your life, leaving you feeling fragmented, stuck, or confused. Each one of us carries a personal story, a past that continuously influences our present.

In this section, we'll be exploring our thought patterns and feelings, peeling back the layers to understand their origins and impacts. In each chapter, I'll present a question for you to sit with. These questions are invitations to introspection, designed to encourage you to pause and reflect deeply. I believe this practice is an essential part of the healing process, as it allows you to connect with your inner self, understand your experiences, and ease you into this healing journey.

We depend on others for our happiness

My first recollection of heartbreak was when I was four years old. My grandfather told me he didn't love me. I still remember the initial confusion as I tried to process the emotions I felt. Yes, I was hurt but this pain was new; it felt like my heart had split into two.

It was my first week of school, a time that's usually filled with the joys of making friends and learning new things. My mum couldn't pick me up that day, due to work commitments, so my grandfather showed up instead. I was eager to tell him about my day and all the wonderful things that had happened. But his reply, spoken in a heavy Trinidadian accent, was simply, 'I doh care bout that.' Grandad was always miserable, so I didn't pay him much mind. However, when we reached home, the atmosphere grew heavier. I was still in high spirits, so I continued talking and following him around. That's when he knelt down, looked me squarely in the eyes, and said, 'I doh care bout that. I doh love you. Hush your mouth and go wait for your mudda to come.'

I ran to the living room and curled up in the corner of the couch. Waiting for my mum felt like an eternity – every minute that passed was riddled with confusion and all that consumed my mind was the simple question: *What did I do wrong?*

That's my first core memory, and it's a harsh one, isn't it? Even though it's tough to carry, it's played a significant role in forming how I view certain things. This experience made it clear how complex human emotions and relationships can be. As painful as it was, it served as a stark lesson: Love isn't always a guarantee, even when you think it should be – especially when it comes to family, your first community, who are naturally expected to offer unconditional love and protection.

You see, my grandfather was an abusive man and the brunt of his anger, unfortunately, fell on my mother. Witnessing that abuse as a child was both heartbreaking and eye-opening. The relationship I had with my mother, Janette, was the bedrock on which my life was built. She was my world, and our bond was my sanctuary. She was a remarkable woman, but not just because of the unconditional love she poured into me. She also showed incredible strength when life got tough. Despite her difficult past, she became a living example of what it means to overcome.

Even with the heavy baggage of her history, my mother became a symbol of resilience and independence. She single-handedly raised me after breaking away from my father, who was neither present nor a positive influence in our lives. Her role as a bookkeeper enabled her to offer me a better future. She poured both time and resources into my upbringing, giving me opportunities she'd never had.

What struck me most was her sacrifice of personal time. As a single mother, her moments of solitude or leisure were rare. Despite this, Mum made sure she had some alone time in the mornings and evenings – a non-negotiable that I not only respected but also incorporated into my daily routine and something I still do to this day. There were the occasional times, too, when she'd hire a babysitter and go out with her friends for the night. I would sit at the end of her bed in awe, captivated by the transformation as she dressed up. The air would fill with the scent of her signature perfume, Poison, and for a moment, she looked stress-free, glowing in her happiness.

In my eyes, it was always us two against the world. My mother's life was far from easy, but her spirit, her resilience, and her love shaped me into who I am today. And for that, I am eternally grateful.

Born just off Coffee Street – or 'the Coffee' – in San Fernando, Trinidad and Tobago, my mum experienced a childhood filled with the love of communal living. She was raised by her grandmother, Evelyn, and grew up in a wooden house, which she shared with her siblings, aunts, and uncles. It was a humble but happy upbringing. Evelyn would divide everything she bought into four and share it among her grandchildren. There was so much love in that home, they didn't even realize they were poor.

Her life, however, took a dramatic turn at the age of 16 when she reunited with her parents in England, who had left years earlier during the Windrush era. What should have been a heartfelt reunion quickly turned into a nightmare. You see, Mum's parents – my grandparents – were not your average set of parents. They were narcissistic and thrived on the cruel practices of division and manipulation.

The family home was not a sanctuary, but instead a battleground where psychological and other kinds of abuse would take place throughout the day. Beatings were frequent. In fact, on the day of my mum's arrival, she was brutally beaten and forced to scrub the kitchen floor. When she finished, she was shown her bedroom. As she unpacked, she looked out the window and was captivated by the unique architecture that differed from what she'd known back home. For the first time, she saw rows of terraced houses stretching into the distance and described it as a maze she could never escape from. This became her first memory of England.

As the eldest child, my mum carried an unfair share of responsibilities and burdens. Her roles in the family dynamic were both scapegoat and caretaker. This was the harsh reality she faced growing up, completely different from her nostalgic memories of Trinidad. Yet her spirit remained unbroken. As the years passed, she liberated herself from that house and rebuilt a new life for herself; one that included a respectable job, friends that felt like sisters, and, finally, starting a family of her own. But leaving her family home didn't free her immediately from the emotional and mental ties that connected her to her family. It took many years for her to fully break free from damage that had overshadowed her life.

Breaking free from family dysfunction

Growing up, I witnessed my mother's struggle with her family firsthand. She extended grace repeatedly, even when they hurt her and let her down time and again. My aunts leaned on her heavily but reciprocated neither her love nor her respect. They took advantage of her kindness, disrespected her, and belittled her, leaving her feeling isolated and emotionally drained. All she ever wanted was to replicate the happy family environment she had known growing up in Trinidad. To achieve this, she made herself constantly available to her sisters, even when it took an emotional toll on her.

I could see how sad she'd become after interacting with them. She sought therapy to better her situation and, for a while, it seemed like she was on a path to healing. But then, inevitably, a phone call would pull her back into the toxic loop, triggering the same painful cycle all over again. As a child, I would feel conflicted. A part of me hoped that, maybe this time, they would treat her differently, while another part begged her not to respond. She always felt obligated to show up and support them, and would often say, 'What can I do? They're my family.'

To bring some joy and light into her life, I did what I could to make her smile. I learned to tell jokes just to hear her laugh. I perfected my writing skills and wrote her short stories every day after school for her to read in the evenings. She loved me abundantly; all I wanted was to see her happy.

It wasn't until she reached the age of 60 that my mum started to direct the love and attention she had been giving to her family toward herself. I'll tell you more about this journey later. As for my grandfather, two decades passed before I saw him again. The day he decided to speak his truth was the turning point. When my mum came to collect me, she sensed that something was wrong and took immediate action. She removed me from that harmful environment without hesitation. She stood up, protected, and fought for me, and in that moment, I realized I could confide in her about anything. That experience solidified my trust in her and emphasized her commitment to me and my well-being.

The people-pleasing trap

When we're young, it's natural for us to look to others for our own sense of happiness. I was fortunate to have a loving mum who formulated a nurturing community filled with love and genuine connections. So, I never felt the absence of my extended biological family. I learned early on that they were incapable of demonstrating healthy forms of love and didn't possess the ability to even receive, honor, or experience genuine love. All I ever witnessed was my mum's commitment to supporting her family, with no reciprocation.

And so, I became a reflection of her habits, because what we see and experience repeatedly eventually cements itself into our subconscious and profoundly shapes us into who we are.

Without intervention, the impact of our upbringing can last a lifetime, shaping our behaviors, our values, and even our emotional boundaries.

For most of my life, I was stuck in a cycle of people-pleasing and depending on others to bring joy into my life. The thought of enforcing boundaries scared me because I genuinely believed it would make people leave. I found it difficult to accept help, gifts, or anything without feeling a deep need to reciprocate immediately. This led me to overcompensate by being too readily available, as if my worth depended on how quickly I could respond to others. My phone allowed others full access to me, and I complied every time a notification appeared. Pulling away from my own needs, I fell deeper into the obligations I felt I had toward other people. But this wasn't just about availability – I wanted to be a savior for those who struggled to ask for help. I empathized so deeply that I stepped into the role of becoming their hero without being asked. This made me feel valued, so I never saw a reason to say *no*.

But over time, this constant search for external validation didn't result in me feeling happy or fulfilled. Prioritizing others over myself led to waves of emotional exhaustion, which manifested in my feeling drained and unappreciated, and further contributed to my insecurities. I fell in love with the *potential* of others and dedicated years of my life trying to 'save' people, which resulted in codependency and abusive scenarios. I realized I was giving more than I was receiving and, eventually, I started to learn the value of putting myself first and establishing clear boundaries.

Unravel the patterns of codependency: Put yourself first

It's natural to look for community in others, but not to the detriment of ourselves. Many of us have clung to relationships that we should have let go of, looking for approval and acceptance from others, while sacrificing parts of ourselves in the process. When we feel incomplete, it's tempting to believe that receiving love from someone else will fill that void, as if their compassion can heal us more than our own. So, we go to great lengths just to feel loved – but that's not love; it's dependence, and it's not a healthy way to live.

Have you ever ignored your own needs, just to make someone else feel happy, even if it feels like you're betraying yourself?

That feeling of betrayal is a gentle warning from your intuition, alerting you that the choices you're making are not in alignment with your intentions. You're not being true to yourself and, in turn, you're slipping into the same pattern of putting others above yourself. It's time to stop breaking your own heart and start putting yourself first.

We believe the myth of 'perfection'

My obsession with perfectionism held me back and hindered me from achieving the level of success I knew I could reach. I know, for many, it may not seem that deep – but allow me to explain.

Growing up, I was quite a handful and far from an easy child to raise. The early years at my first primary school were turbulent. School was my first real exposure to the outer world (beyond the trickles of what my family had already shown me), and what I saw infuriated me to my core. Why was I the only kid without a dad? Why couldn't Mum pick me up from school? Why wasn't there anyone at the gates eagerly waiting to collect me? The more I noticed, the angrier I became. This manifested as me becoming the class bully. I would terrorize the kids who had the things that I lacked.

My behavior took a toll on my mum. She became so overwhelmed that she even extended her hours at work, spending more money on childcare, just to avoid the inevitable arguments that would greet her when she got home. I was angry, but my anger was warranted. I'm the type of person who hates being kept in the dark. I need to be made aware of all the details, so I can form my own conclusions; otherwise, I'll continually be searching for the truth. I felt discarded due to my father's absence – a man who, as my mum later discovered, was notorious for walking away from his (multiple) families.

I never met my father. From a young age, I had a premonition that our first meeting would be at his funeral, and lo and behold, I was right. I watched his funeral on YouTube while I was stranded in Trinidad during the pandemic. Was I sad that he died? Well, ask yourself this: When was the last time you mourned a complete stranger?

But I admit I was curious about him. For the first time, I wondered about the sound of his laugh and the tone of his voice. Did he have an accent like Mum's? He was funny, apparently – I wondered how he expressed his humor. I wondered if we had any similar mannerisms. Not once, however, did I regret not meeting him. The best thing my father did for me was leave Mum and me alone. Other siblings of mine are emotionally wounded from his sporadic visits, broken promises, and long disappearing acts, but I managed to avoid it all.

Throughout my life, Mum spoke highly of my father. They were friends for years, so she had many beautiful stories about him. She loved him. He'd made her happy at one stage, and I was planned and conceived in love. Mum would always reinforce the similarities we had and attributed my creativity to him. As I got older, my anger toward him transformed into utter disappointment for his failure to be the man he should have been.

I've often pondered why he created families only to abandon them. Part of me wonders if he was discovering different parts of himself with each relationship. Another part sees it as sheer irresponsibility and a lack of self-awareness. He didn't just walk away – he built lives, married, and bought houses, perhaps to keep doors open for a possible return.

The truth hit my mother hard when she was pregnant and engaged to him. An aunt revealed he was already married with three other sons. Following his exposure, he became violent and unpredictable. Eventually, my mother chose a peaceful life for us and cut ties with him. My mum struggled with how to deliver this truth without breaking my heart. But as time went on, she realized that this was a conversation that needed to happen.

A fresh start

My disruptive behavior ultimately led to my exclusion from school. This, however, was the beginning of a positive shift in my life, although I didn't realize it at the time.

Not to excuse my behavior, but if I reflect honestly, that primary school had its share of turmoil. The environment was often disorderly, mirroring the chaos in the classrooms. This influenced my behavior for the worse. My friend Mo, of Pakistani descent, would share swear words from his language with me. There was an incident that I'll never forget, where a woman physically dragged me through the frozen food aisle in Sainsbury's, and angrily confronted my mum. She demanded to know where I had learned such words, after I'd told her 'to go shit herself.' I genuinely didn't know that *that* was what I'd said! These experiences were pivotal for my mum. She was determined that my next school would have a stronger foundation in ethics, education, and discipline. And that's how I ended up at Sacred Heart.

Transitioning to the Catholic school environment of Sacred Heart was a shock to my system. Everything felt unfamiliar. There were rigorous rules and a highly intentional structure; for the first time, my inappropriate behavior in school wasn't tolerated. The first morning Mass I attended was an experience, to say the least. I snuck into the cupboards and ate all the Holy Communion wafers. (In my defense, I was starving, and I thought they were crackers.) Unsurprisingly, I got into trouble, and the disciplinary action resulted in my mum being called in. The school knew I had challenges with adapting, but they were committed to helping me adjust. On the way home, my mum sighed and said, 'Meggan, girl, this is a fresh start. Behave well, get a good first report, and there'll be a surprise waiting for you.'

I could sense my mum's exhaustion over my behavior and knew this was a new incentive for me to start acting right. Plus, Mum always gave thoughtful gifts, so I decided to comply and made changes overnight. The transformation was swift and within a few weeks, my behavior had remarkably improved. The day she picked me up from school became a significant core memory – and not just because her doing so was a rare occurrence. As I climbed into the car, I saw an envelope on the passenger seat. Inside was a handwritten letter, congratulating me for such a successful first term, and tickets to go and see Michael Jackson that night at Wembley Stadium. I nearly combusted!

That experience did more than make me happy. It planted a seed within that laid the foundation for a newfound confidence and heightened my self-belief. I started to develop faith in my abilities. It showed me the benefits of good behavior and the rewards that followed when you choose to act accordingly. It was a beautiful lesson to learn. As time passed, however, simply 'being good' tipped over into something else. Perfectionism began to consume me and, to be honest, that battle is partly still with me today.

The root of my perfectionism

The mission to become perfect stemmed from multiple times in my life where I was rewarded for being anything other than my authentic self. I learned how to perform and spent years beneath this disguise – so much so that I struggled to develop a real relationship with my authentic self. I became everything everyone wanted me to be.

I knew my extended family were incapable of loving me, because of their disdain toward my mum, so from a young age, I just learned to stop searching for their love. However, despite numbing this feeling, I still had moments where I yearned to be loved and accepted just like my cousins were. Seeing them showered with attention and expensive gifts at Christmases and birthdays, I couldn't help but compare myself unfavorably. So in my bid to receive the same affection from my aunts that I saw my cousins receiving, I did all I could to be the 'ideal child' among my family.

As I grew older, and social media's influence became more ingrained in my daily experience, the comparisons escalated. I would scroll through feeds of influencers' highlight reels and believed that I couldn't advance in my career until I matched their aesthetic. I would think, *I should be more like this person or that person, but I'm not even close – look at my hair, my weight, my house, my personality. None of it meets this standard.* All these reasons held me back.

For years, I allowed the pursuit of perfection to stifle my growth and I let many opportunities pass me by. This mindset usually stems from trauma, which causes you to carry the belief that you must attain a level of perfection to be worthy of love. Interestingly, the journey toward healing counteracts that idea.

In the healing process, we're in a constant state of evolution, discovering new ways to refine ourselves.

As our healing unfolds in real time, we embrace our imperfections along the way, until all is resolved. This is proof that you don't have to wait for everything to be 'perfect' to move forward. Life simply doesn't operate like that.

Redefining 'perfect' and embracing imperfection

The pain of missing opportunities taught me a fundamental lesson: nobody has it all figured out. We're all on this journey of learning, stumbling, reemerging, and growing every single day. Even the people we admire are works in progress, evolving at their own pace. It's OK to have off days, but pretending to be the complete, finished version of yourself is not.

Our idea of perfection is flawed; we measure ourselves against others, without recognizing that we're all walking a unique path that was destined solely for us to pursue. We will never find our true essence by emulating someone else. Because while they're naturally living in their truth, we neglect our magic by mirroring their methods, hoping to have a life like theirs. It's such a devastating form of self-betrayal.

We're commonly told that life is not a rehearsal, but in cases like these, I beg to differ. When we view life as a rehearsal, it liberates us from the fear of making mistakes and instead, invites us to embrace the notion that every step or misstep that we take is part of a larger process of becoming. There's no such thing as failure, and no need for competition or comparison. By adopting this perspective, we give ourselves the freedom to find our true essence, where the pursuit for authenticity is valued over the pursuit of flawlessness. This releases us from the need to replicate another person's journey. When you look at life as a rehearsal, you can keep trying and refining until you get it right and then move on to the next chapter.

So, what does that say about our need to be perfect? The energy and time we pour into this pursuit is ultimately a waste of time.

Perfection is an unattainable goal. It has nothing to do with our ability – it simply doesn't exist. It's a myth, a construct that we desperately need to detach ourselves from.

Think about it: My idea of 'perfect' was never based on a universal truth. Instead, it was influenced by my opinion and the things that have shaped me along the way. From beauty standards, material possessions, and the curated feeds I digested daily on social media, I created a vision of what I deemed 'perfect' should look like. But the thing is, we humans define perfection in so many different ways that it can't possibly exist as an absolute truth.

For one person, a perfect life might involve living extravagantly in a huge mansion, complete with a couple of Rolls Royces parked in the driveway (slowly raises hand). For another, it might be moving away and living remotely in their ideal location, while working on something they're passionate about. And that's perfectly fine. For every house that's considered an architectural masterpiece, there's someone who'll look at it and think, *Ew, absolutely not – that's awful!* And again, there's nothing wrong with that. My idea of a perfect day is adventuring through the forests in Trinidad and stumbling upon a new waterfall, cleansing away the old energies I've been storing with a bar of blue soap, while my friends are somewhere close, creating a fire to cook a pot of curry. I love the simple life, with a trickle of luxury. And it's just that: *my* vision. It doesn't have to be anyone else's. So, it's ridiculous to maintain such a subjective and ever-changing standard that is 'perfection.'

Our idea of perfection is flawed; we measure ourselves against others, without recognizing that we're all walking a unique path that was destined solely for us to pursue. We will never find our true essence by emulating someone else.

**The universe doesn't require us to be perfect;
in fact, the universe itself is a living testament
to the beauty that can be found in imperfection.**

Trees grow to different heights, some grow crooked, others straight. The moon goes through her phases. Water is never consistent – sometimes it's peaceful, other times it's crashing against the rocks as if it's having a war within. Even the sky presents us with a different masterpiece each evening. We don't even acknowledge the anomalies; we just marvel at their existence and feel grateful to be able to witness such beauty. It's a pity we don't extend this sense of awe inward – I often wonder why we look at the world's phenomena and forget to include ourselves.

Celebrate your authentic self

Perfectionism is a trap that sabotages our growth, and we need to stop feeding into it. Chasing perfection is dangerous because we're constantly perpetuating the idea that we're not worthy of being ourselves. We mold ourselves into different forms, changing – rather than embracing – the abundance of our true character.

We should make a pact to start celebrating our authentic selves. Unapologetically. I know who I am: cheeky and dynamic, a bit rude, and a bit vibrant. That's me! The more I love that authentic self, the more I'll flourish and grow as a human being. It's a work in progress. The only way to liberate ourselves from our attachment to perfectionism is by appreciating what's already perfect right here, in the present.

You are whole, you are complete, just as you are.

You are an embodiment of your past, present, and future combined. Even when we feel like we don't quite fit in, trusting in our unique qualities and strengths deepens our self-reliance and our inner connection. Understand this: Your true self doesn't need 'improvement' because it continually evolves. The real work is aligning with who you already are.

And to clarify, I'm not saying that embracing authenticity means that I reject the idea of personal growth or betterment. Being true to ourselves involves recognizing and accepting who we are at this moment, while acknowledging that we have the potential and the right to evolve into a more fulfilling version of ourselves. It's allowing ourselves to know that we're able to grow into something more, while still being content with where we currently stand.

Do you ever find yourself obsessing about attaining an ideal of perfection, and chiding yourself for coming up short?

We must recognize the dangers of chasing the unattainable and lean more toward appreciating our genuine selves. Yes, there will always be parts of ourselves that we refine, but let's not get caught up in the never-ending pursuit of perfection. It doesn't exist. So, let's move forward.

We follow other people's visions for our lives instead of our own

In hindsight, I should never have attended university. But as a child of a migrant, I knew how important education was and I didn't want to disappoint. Little did I know, I'd take greater pride in following my own path than in conforming to family expectations.

There's a heavy expectation that surrounds first-generation children of migrants and immigrants – even more so if you were privileged enough to return home and witness for yourself the differences there compared to 'living abroad.' As much as the pressure to succeed hovers over you, there's a deep sense of pride, honor, and gratitude for the sacrifices our parents or grandparents made for the promise of living a 'better life.'

Some of us were born to parents who understood the value of exploration. They recognized that their sacrifices weren't just about immediate success, but also about granting us the freedom to wander and to find our true calling amid the possibilities that surrounded us. Conversely, others had parents who were more focused on steering us toward specialized roles, where the expectation of receiving accolades and higher achievements was the standard.

Growing up, I witnessed close relatives sabotage their children's opportunities out of fear of losing control over them. They had a vision of the life they wanted their children to live, and as a result, they ruined any chance for their children's talents to be nurtured and developed. This caused their children to grow into adults who found it difficult to trust their own voices.

How we become disconnected

In a lot of ways, it's hardly surprising that many of us ended up disconnected from our goals and aspirations. From an early age, we were conditioned to chase dreams that weren't entirely our own. Unfortunately, in this life, there's a script we must follow – you go to school, you follow the rules – but what happens when the rules no longer align with who you're growing into? When I reached secondary school, this internal conflict became something I struggled with daily. I would thrive in the subjects that ignited my passions and abscond from the rest. Why should I waste my time studying French when I wanted to learn Spanish?

My 'disconnect' didn't go unnoticed. Mr. P., my head of year, became vexed at my selective approach. 'What's going on, Meggan?' he would ask, clearly frustrated, yet concerned. 'Why don't you apply the same level of enthusiasm to all of your subjects, like you do with art?'

Although Mr. P. was fair, he was also strict, and as my list of lunchtime detentions continued to grow longer, a solution had to be found. Missing lessons was beginning to affect my overall attendance, which was non-negotiable for my mum. Mr. P. reiterated that regardless of whether I saw myself living a conventional life or not, I still needed to leave school with good grades. So, we came to an agreement: He would alter my timetable so that I could attend more of the classes I enjoyed, but I had to promise to attend at least one class a week for the subjects I hated.

Meeting Mr. P. halfway was a small step toward solidifying my autonomy, but it was short-lived. Once school ended, attending college and university was mandatory in my household. Education was of prime importance to Mum. When she migrated, she worked diligently in a factory, cutting fabric for a clothing company. She prided herself on obtaining a higher education, which enabled her to gain access to better opportunities. Mum always jokingly reminded me, 'It's either you get a good education and create the life you want, or you marry a rich man.' This was something her grandmother would always say to her. Lord knows, a man wouldn't be able to contain me. I'm too much of a free spirit. He'd kick me out! So, the only option was the education route. When I got accepted into university, my mum couldn't have been prouder but, internally, I was conflicted.

From the first day on campus, I felt out of place. While my friends from college effortlessly found their communities, I struggled to connect with anyone. I began to feel isolated. It might sound trivial, but as my mum helped me move into my dorm, I burst into tears. I despised everything: the course, the environment, the rapid pace at which my life was changing. The shift was happening way too fast, and I wasn't ready to step out of my comfort zone. Then I met a girl called Toni. Our paths crossed in the shared kitchen as I tried to explore my surroundings. Before she could even introduce herself, I burst into tears *again*.

As she comforted me, all I could think was, *you can't keep crying like this. Please – just make a decision.* Things didn't improve as time went on. I ended up repeating the first year almost three times, repeatedly breaking my own heart by ignoring my spirit's urges to leave.

I spent years of my life paralyzed by fear. I'd been living in the shadows of other people's expectations for so long and it had led me nowhere, except to a deep state of unhappiness. I was depressed and miserable. My early 20s were anxiety-inducing; I was drifting aimlessly, in a state of limbo, without a plan or a vision. I took a break from uni and returned home, to more familiar surroundings, where I could articulate my thoughts and determine what my next steps would be. I didn't miss education, but I did miss the routine. The life I'd been so accustomed to living was slowly fading away. After weeks of feeling sorry for myself, stuck in my bedroom, crying down the walls like Usher in his music videos, I finally plucked up the courage to speak to Mum about how I was feeling. 'I've tried my best,' I told her, 'but university just isn't for me.'

Initially, she was disappointed over the time and money invested, and she became deeply concerned about my mental state. Yet, almost immediately after, she shifted into a form of genuine support and reassurance. She said, 'Why didn't you say something sooner? If you have a plan, you will always have my support. If you're not happy baby, just stop.' In that moment, it struck me, and my first thought was *Shit, why* didn't *I speak up earlier?* It wasn't like my household environment discouraged transparency. The real issue was me. I was trapped in a cycle of trying to live up to my community's expectations – so much so that I'd convinced myself university was the only path worth pursuing.

My turning point

That heart-to-heart with my mum was a pivotal moment that shifted my entire perspective on life. It taught me that there was no need to rush, overthink, or stagnate.

Life is a journey that is meant to flow freely as we continue to evolve organically.

What is meant to be will be. The only real obligation we have is to remain true to our calling and committed to the work that needs to be done to move forward. That conversation was the first step toward crafting and respecting my vision for my life.

However, what followed shortly after wasn't as straightforward as I'd hoped. There was a series of highs and lows. Stepping into the real world while most of my friends were still studying was a lonely and frightening experience. I was directionless, struggling to figure out how to bring forth the ideas I envisioned. I felt inadequate.

For six long months, depression stayed by my side, and I isolated myself in my room, distracting myself from the consequences of my choices. It got bad. It was a dark period, but deep down, I knew this was a challenge I had to overcome to get to the other side. So, I made a conscious effort to shift my mindset and embrace the season. I indulged myself in YouTube documentaries that focused on how other people had turned their low points into catalysts for change, and this daily 'indoctrination' slowly began to change my outlook on my own situation. I realized that hardships are usually the soil in which personal development grows and that this was the moment I'd been called to start planting seeds.

Finding our own path

We need to break free and stop residing in the boxes of other people's expectations. There is always the temptation to surrender our natural calling, causing us to default on our journey to self-discovery.

It's impossible to meet your genuine self when you're constantly under the shadow of someone else's expectations.

This may come across as morbid, but one of the most common regrets people share on their deathbeds is that they suppressed their true selves – they put their dreams second, and ignored the inner voice that urged them to explore life on their terms. Hearing such confessions from those approaching the end of their lives is both heartbreaking and enlightening. In that moment, the clarity they offer is invaluable.

Imagine knowing you're about to step into the unknown, leaving behind this earthly experience, and the only piece of advice you wish to share is the importance of living life to the fullest. How can that not wake you up? We so easily give away our freedom to experience a beautiful life, simply because we fear what others will say. We fear the scrutiny and judgment from those who are also caught in this trap and struggling. It's a mess, and at some point, someone must break the mold.

It's also important to note that when people impose their expectations onto us, they aren't always coming from a place of malice. Many of our elders often had no choice but to conform to societal norms, regardless of how they felt. It's a sad realization when you consider how many unfulfilled dreams are lying dormant in cemeteries across the world. We're fortunate to be living in such a transformative time; where we have access to freedoms that were once perceived as unattainable. I think we should all utilize those freedoms to the best of our ability – if not for ourselves, then in honor of those who came before us.

> So, what's the first step? How do we move toward following our own vision, and detaching from the expectations of others?

By being honest, first with ourselves, and then extending that honesty to others. Then by having the courage to stand by our choices, no matter how challenging it gets. We're all guilty of maintaining habits that don't serve our best interests, and letting go of those attachments takes time. So, patience is paramount. Mistakes and reoccurrences are bound to happen. But they shouldn't prevent you from reclaiming your power as you grow beyond the outdated version of yourself, refusing to succumb to external pressures.

It takes courage to amplify your voice and go against the grain.

I regretted not having that conversation with my mum sooner. Every time the Student Loan Company deducts money from my wages, I want to cry. But that's the price I must pay for choosing to walk down a path that wasn't aligned with me. However, that very decision changed the trajectory of my life and I'm eternally grateful for the courage I had back then. One thing I'll never regret is staying true to myself.

We all deserve the freedom to explore the unknowns, unburdened by the expectations of others. There are no rules that require us to conform. Regret, unhappiness, and misery can all be avoided if you learn to live in accordance with your own vision. Detaching ourselves from the expectations of others is the only way we're going to start to find ourselves – and being able to do so is a privilege that we should all embrace.

We stay in our comfort zones out of fear of the unknown

Getting in my own way is a journey I know all too well. There have been numerous times in my life when I've let my comfort zone stop me from moving forward.

Take, for example, the moment I decided to leave university. After that conversation with Mum, I didn't just dive back into work. I spiraled into a six-month season of depression, feeling completely lost and devoid of value. I spent days aimlessly wandering around my flat, disappointing my mother and wasting time on endless distractions. But I was paralyzed by fear and apprehensive about stepping into an uncertain future.

Fear had a hold on me, and it felt like my life was consumed by it. I would have these vivid dreams and visions of executing the work that needed to be done. But as soon as I was required to step out of my comfort zone, my pursuit of those dreams would end abruptly. Fear for me manifested as this invisible barricade, secured by guards whose main role was to reinforce the idea that I was incapable.

So, I understand how exhausting it is to spend our days envisioning a life for ourselves and not having the confidence to pursue it.

The turning point came when my mother told me it was time to find employment. I ended up working in a prison – a far cry from my previous gig at Foot Locker. But despite its challenges, something deep within told me this experience would be invaluable.

First, directly witnessing the impact on the inmates of losing their liberty served as an undeniable wake-up call. Second, it was at that job that I discovered my ability to uplift others through affirmations and consistent encouragement. I helped one inmate improve his relationship with his grandmother by stressing the importance of presenting yourself well. He would attend visitations looking scruffy and this would cause his grandmother great distress. The moment he braided his hair and changed his attire, she rejoiced and broke down in tears. I also encouraged inmates to utilize the library, suggesting they use their remaining time inside for self-education, to enhance their chances of betterment when they were released. I tried to help people rehabilitate themselves.

This chapter of my life taught me the power of stepping out of my comfort zone and embracing the unknown. It's a struggle that can resonate with many.

Confronting the fear of change

We've all seen people close to us demonstrate the realities of what happens when you're scared to embrace change. Their indecisiveness is evident as they waver between letting go of their old ways and reverting to the very habits that kept them stuck in the first place. In the process, they lose sight of their initial intentions, making any attempt to move forward seem unachievable.

I've seen people remain loyal to their sadness, making it last longer than it should and allowing it to become a part of their identity, simply because the journey toward healing seemed daunting or required too many lifestyle alterations. Others have adopted a similar stance toward the shifts and challenges that life throws at us all and chosen escapism instead of confrontation. Change is rarely easy. It can feel painful before it feels good. Whether it's changing our mindset, habits, or energy, transformations are usually uncomfortable at first.

Look beneath your comfort-zone habits and ask yourself: What are you *really* afraid of?

At the core, the source of our hesitancy is simply a deep essence of fear. We're afraid to step outside our comfort zones and, as sad as it sounds, we're intimidated by the magnitude of our own personal power. We're scared to commit to ourselves, to embrace the solitude that's required to achieve change. We're anxious about how others will perceive us, about rejection, fearful of facing negative encounters. We're embarrassed to be seen as a failure, and of having to deal with the humiliation that follows a setback. Even love, in its purest form – receiving and returning – is terrifying for some.

When we allow our comfort zones to hold us captive, we essentially put limits on our human experience. The fear plagues our inner dialogue, convincing us that our evolution is unnecessary, which in turn plants seeds of self-doubt. It causes us to become preoccupied with 'what

Standing in our pain is no easier than taking the steps to move ahead. The comfort zone was never intended to be a place for us to build permanent foundations.

if?' scenarios, and diverts our focus from the present moment, and what we can do to improve our current situation. When we feel like a failure, we behave like one.

Language as a catalyst for change

The great news is, we can shift this fear by altering the language we use when communicating with ourselves. This initial step is crucial for moving beyond the fear that keeps us bound to our comfort zones.

We all have the capability to navigate through the unknown, whether that means leaving a toxic relationship, breaking a harmful habit, or simply trying something new that scares us.

You have the power to take yourself down this uncharted path. When I realized that the traditional nine-to-five life wasn't for me, I found inspiration from the stories of others – entrepreneurs, writers, business owners – who had all succeeded by defying societal norms. They are brave and fearless – but so are we. You deserve to explore a life that may seem intimidating at first. On the other side is a version of you that can only be accessed through the conviction of overcoming your fears.

In fact, I think we need to reframe the phrase 'comfort zone' – because there's nothing truly comfortable about it, right? It's a space of *discomfort* that often leaves us feeling unhappy. Comfort is something that makes you feel good and nurtured, not sad, detached, and fearful. I hated every moment of being stagnant: the guilt, the lethargy, the lack of attention and motivation. However, the loss of time and interest in the things I was passionate about were the parts I grieved the most.

If you're struggling with fear of the unknown, just keep this in mind: The only way we can reveal and heal the uncomfortable truths that lie beneath the surface is to face the fears that come with implementing positive changes in our lives. Standing in our pain is no easier than taking the steps to move ahead. The comfort zone was never intended to be a place for us to build permanent foundations.

We lose sight of ourselves and our purpose

Please be advised: This chapter includes sensitive content related to suicide. Please proceed with care if you find this topic triggering.

Have you ever experienced that sense of not recognizing yourself at all? You look in the mirror at your reflection and you simply don't know who that person is looking back? It's you, but not you, deep down?

There's a disconnect between your soul and yourself, and inside you're in turmoil, even if you're coming across to others as completely fine. I know that feeling. It can feel like the worst place to be, emotionally and mentally, when you and your spirit don't align. For me, losing myself came after one of the biggest losses of my life.

I was only 15, and in many ways, it was a beautiful time in my life. The only thing I had to concern myself with was maintaining my good attendance at school and ensuring my homework was handed in on time. Everything was just simple. Social media didn't exist. High school was almost coming to an end, and I was surrounded by so many friends. There was one friend who always used to encourage me to write and make music – Kyle Davis. He was a bit of a rebel at heart but had a soft center. I remember looking outside the window during math class, and there he'd be, cycling around the school grounds on his BMX, while the teachers ran after him. He didn't even attend my school.

One night, during the Easter holiday, there was an event in our local town called Eskimo Dance, where Grime artists from across London would perform and compete. Everyone in the area used to look forward to it, as it was the perfect opportunity to meet new people and have a good time. The night before, a big group of us went to a funfair and we'd started to make plans for the following night. Kyle planned to wear the Prada tracksuit that he'd recently bought. That night we waited until midnight for Kyle to arrive, but he never came.

This wasn't like him, as the Eskimo Dance was his favorite event to attend. I went to the bathroom to use my phone and walked into a frenzy of people on the floor, crying, and doors slamming. One of my friends was screaming: *Kyle's killed himself! He's killed himself!*

The horrendous news flew around our crowd. I went into complete shock. My mum came to pick me up, and I remember looking out of the car window and thinking, *Somebody I know has died.* I was so young; it was almost as if I didn't realise you *could* die. I couldn't work it out. I was so confused. None of it made sense to me.

The impact of Kyle's death on me, on all of us kids, was huge. I became desensitized and numb to the world and started wearing black. I was good friends with a girl called Hannah, and we would go to the morgue every day after school and talk to Kyle as he lay peacefully. When he was buried, we proceeded to visit his grave every day after school. I slept in my mum's bed every night for months. I felt as if the Meggan I had been died that day and as if everyone around me had changed, too.

I didn't know who I was anymore. All of us who were Kyle's friends had lost something in ourselves and to find ourselves again, we had to find a purpose.

How we lose ourselves

My experience was extreme, but it's not just grief that can cause you to lose who you are – I've seen it happen in all kinds of different ways.

A close friend of mine almost lost herself to an eight-year relationship, from the ages of 19 to 27, just as she was becoming an adult and learning how to formulate her narrative. There was a noticeable difference in her energy; she transformed from a confident, sweet, free-spirited, bubbly person to a dimmed version of her true self. Her boyfriend subjected her to so many levels of abuse and manipulation, which affected her confidence and resulted in her dealing with insecurities that she'd never experienced before. It was horrible to watch. Although the relationship had its share of happy moments, he would abuse her in subtle ways, so over time she didn't notice how much he broke her down. It was only after she finally left that relationship, and hit her version of rock bottom, that she realized she no longer recognized the person she'd become and could see how far she'd strayed from herself.

When we don't recognize ourselves, it's time to heal

It's taken a long time, but over the years, I've proudly watched my friend take the time and do the work to return to herself. There were evenings when I would visit her, and we'd talk for hours. In her healing journey, she developed a heightened self-awareness, which enabled her to come to terms with how she'd let herself down during that relationship.

She would reflect on the efforts she'd made to receive love from him, only to realize that he was incapable of providing her with the emotional maturity and safety that she deserved. Or when she was able to pinpoint the day the abuse began but didn't dare to do anything about it. Having never encountered that level of emotional abuse before, she'd lacked the life experience to know how to deal with it.

As she healed, she stopped dating and started to achieve things outside of romantic relationships. She spent more time with friends and developed healthier boundaries. She used to be the sort of person who'd say, 'Sure, you can come over at 11 p.m.' and now she's stopped doing that. It's so beautiful to watch her develop her sense of self-love, but it's still a work in progress.

These experiences have shown me that it's always possible to return home to yourself. Even if you are in the depths of destructive habits and feel unable to move beyond your current state.

Do you feel like you're in the depths of destructive habits and don't recognize who you've become?

Self-sabotage is such a common way that we break our own hearts. Self-sabotage involves behaviors that both harm us and prevent us from moving forward. It's a form of learned behavior that we adopt due to our past traumas. When we're in the presence of those who promote an attachment to unhealthy habits, as my friend did with her boyfriend, over time, this can make its way into our psyche and rewire our minds into accepting self-destructive behaviors as the norm. We come to believe we're inadequate and doubt our ability to make better decisions for our lives.

Breaking the cycle and finding our way back

If we struggle to treat ourselves compassionately, then our behavior will continue to mirror the negative ways in which we view ourselves. It's a vicious cycle, but it can be broken. In the depths of my depression after Kyle's death, I was helped hugely by a mentor called Lincoln Beckford, who created a summer youth academy for the kids in Watford. He created a safe space for us to connect, create, and just be ourselves.

Returning home to ourselves is an art. It's a process that requires us to recall the parts of ourselves that we've buried, rediscovering the value we hold outside of the things that caused us to stray.

It allowed me to heal. It enabled me to leave behind what had happened in high school and move forward.

Returning home to ourselves is an art. It's a process that requires us to recall the parts of ourselves that we've buried, rediscovering the value we hold outside of the things that caused us to stray. By letting go of the negative things that captivated us or the people we held onto, who were slowly depreciating our joy, a bittersweet essence takes over. We finally arrive at a place where we can reconnect with ourselves while simultaneously mourning the time we lost.

We are the source of infinite love.

It's only when we return to this state that we are reminded that love isn't something we experience from time to time, but something we own and produce. The main reason why we stray away from ourselves is because we allow ourselves to lose sight of this truth. After years of devaluing our essence, the first step to returning home to ourselves is letting go of the things that aren't in alignment with our true nature.

We get angry at others for not meeting our expectations

I've touched on this earlier – the self-inflicted heartbreak we endure when we let the expectations of others steer our lives, instead of honoring our dreams and visions. And I will always stand by that. We relinquish all our power when we build our self-worth on the expectations and validation of others.

But we can also harm ourselves by expecting others to live up to *our* standards. I promise this concept is simpler than it appears to be. For a long stretch of my life, I played the role of the 'fixer.' I was the sort of person who was driven by the desire to help others improve their lives, usually to my detriment. I adopted an unhealthy pattern of distributing my time and energy to others, while neglecting my own needs.

One person who I particularly wanted to fix was a dear relative of mine. We were close, but our upbringings were different. The investment from our mothers had no similarities. While I was showered with unconditional love and attention from my mum, they didn't receive the same, and if they did, it was riddled with psychological contradictions that severely impacted them growing up. It's important to note that their mother suffered horrendous levels of trauma as a child, which shaped her into a person unable to give or receive love correctly. But whereas Mum decided to take the opposite path to her own upbringing, their mother didn't. So, in turn, my relative suffered, and consequently developed many destructive traits.

Over the years, I tried everything I could to resolve my relative's problems. From loaning money to exposing them to a range of different opportunities that would have changed the trajectory of their life. I did it with other friends, too: using my platform on social media to lift them up, going into business with them – anything I could do to 'save' them or bring them in, to make their lives better. However, I didn't realize that all these so-called good deeds were simply avoidance tactics on my part. I didn't have the confidence to stay on my own path. I was so scared of being me that I projected all my energy onto other people, convincing myself (and them) that *this* was the path they should follow.

And guess what? It didn't work – not for them or for me. My relative wasn't 'fixed.' Instead, I created a codependent relationship that I had to break away from, and my friends weren't aligned to the path I had put them on, either. Why would they be? They had their own destinies to fulfill, and it wasn't my place to interrupt that progress. Despite my efforts, things didn't improve, and I felt resentful and angry that people weren't responding to the help I was giving them.

Have you ever found yourself in a similar position? Offering unsolicited advice or help, with good intentions of course, and finding yourself feeling frustrated because the outcome isn't what you expected it to be? Have you ever asked yourself where that anger originated from? Maybe this emotion could be a reflection of something within you. The disappointment you're feeling could be a projection of the disappointment you feel toward yourself. Maybe you extended beyond your limits, or invested too much energy into someone else's problem while neglecting your own needs in the process. It's worth taking a moment to question where this emotional turbulence is truly coming from. It's an essential step in understanding the relationship not only with yourself but with others, too.

From projection to personal empowerment

It took more than a decade for me to understand that I was projecting my hopes and dreams onto others, rather than focusing on myself, because it felt easier that way. It felt easier to invest in someone else's potential rather than confront my own. But this understanding eventually crystallized, leading me to the realization that I needed to redirect my energy back toward myself.

I came to understand *it's not my duty to save others*. I also realized that the anger and frustration I felt when others didn't respond to my help was 100 percent a projection!

It's a universal truth that the character traits we don't like in other people, those things that drive us crazy and get us angry, are the character traits we don't like in ourselves.

For example – and this is funny because I'm guilty of this, or at least, I'm known for constantly doing this to others – I would become so irritated and offended at those who didn't honor my time. I *hated* wasting my time. It was the ultimate sign of disrespect. But I'm frequently late! When I take a deeper look, I have such a frivolous relationship with time. I adopted a carefree attitude years ago and learned to brush away the importance of time. But I only felt the brunt of that when others treated me with the same brush.

The reality is, I struggled to maintain my timekeeping and it was something I was highly insecure about. Regardless of what I did, time always seemed to be slipping away from me. That is, until therapy taught me the importance of time blocking. This allowed me to have a deeper sense of control over my life, which drastically improved my timekeeping.

> Do you find yourself consumed with frustration and anger at others when they don't respond the way you think they should?

We avoid ourselves by trying to fix and control others. So, if you're dealing with 'difficult' people in your lives who don't seem grateful and aren't responding to the help you're offering – stop. Turn these emotions around from projecting outward, to inward. Ask yourself the question: Who are you *really* angry at?

We lack self-love and become vulnerable to unhealthy attachments

I've already covered several ways in which we break our own hearts and maybe some of them sound familiar to you.

Depending on others for our own sense of validation, staying in comfort zones that hold us back, projecting our hopes and dreams onto those around us... They might all be different, but there's a common thread that holds them all together, and that's lack of self-love. I honestly believe this is one of the biggest ways in which we break our own hearts, and it lies beneath so many of the destructive behaviors that prevent us from leading a better life.

Have you ever invested in a relationship – whether romantic or platonic – that left you exhausted, emotionally wounded, and questioning your self-worth? Have you got a friend that you know is an incredible person, but who keeps making bad decisions about the people they surround themselves with and invest their time in? I have, and I bet you have, too.

I spoke earlier about my friend who lost her sense of self over many years to a gaslighting boyfriend. My mum lost many years of her life to pouring love into a family that didn't respect her or care about her well-being. I wasted years in my 20s in a terrible relationship with a man who treated me like shit, but I kept going back to him. Underneath all these patterns is a deep-seated belief we aren't worthy of love because we don't love ourselves.

Facing the reality of a toxic relationship

I can now see how fucked-up this relationship I was in truly was – and I understand that I invited it into my life because I was in a fucked-up place myself. My mum knew the relationship was bad for me, and would try to boost me up, saying, 'Don't you know how good you are?' Friends would get frustrated with me because I'd swear up and down that I wasn't going back to him but then get caught literally coming out of his house. (Yup, this happened, and I was so embarrassed! I was driving back from his place in the early hours of the morning, and coincidentally, my friends were on the same road, driving home after an event. What are the odds? They noticed my car and drove behind me, flashing their headlights. I activated the hands-free on my phone as they called me, and they were hysterically laughing at me down the phone. I hung up and continued looking straight ahead as they drove past me. I felt like a complete loser.) But I kept giving him more chances; none of the well-meaning words from my loved ones made any difference.

Deep down, we know when we're being mistreated. I did. Still, when we choose to remain in bad company despite its effect on us, we continue to expose ourselves to distress, frustration, and heartbreak which, ultimately, chip away at our self-worth.

In many ways, this happens unconsciously. Our energy gravitates toward people who reflect it. So, if we're insecure, that's what we attract – insecure people – even if it doesn't look like it on the surface. Manipulative people can sense vulnerability from afar and they'll attach to you like a parasite, drain you, and before you know it, you're in a toxic situation – and it's so hard to get out of.

That's why we need to acknowledge the weight of imbalanced relationships and the hindering effects they have on our personal growth. If we don't love ourselves, we're going to end up around people who don't love us, either.

Breaking free and embracing self-love

The first step to bringing self-love into your life is to recognize that you are worthy. I don't care who you are or where you come from – *everyone* has a light in them that makes them lovable. Telling yourself this is the first step toward changing your internal dialogue, even if you don't believe it at first. When discussing yourself in your internal voice, be mindful of the language you use. No one listens more attentively than you – be kind to and considerate of yourself.

Next, remember that in any type of connection with another human being, mutual respect, support, and genuine compassion are the absolute minimums. Think about the human connections in your life:

- Do they encourage your growth?

- Are they empowering you with their daily habits and commitments?

- Are you engaging in healthy conversations?

- Do they ever leave you questioning your worth?

- Are they kind and supportive during difficult situations?

- Do they uplift and inspire you?

You need to ask yourself: What exactly are you gaining from these connections?

If the answer is 'nothing,' then that's a big red flag. You don't have to be unhappy, and people don't deserve to be in your life by default. That's it. It really is as simple as that. You deserve to be in the presence of those who feel like sunlight.

The truth is, when you value yourself, that's usually when the natural shift takes place, and you begin to let go of the things that no longer serve you and instead gravitate toward those who match your energy. It happened to my friend, my mum, and me, too – eventually. I had to hit rock bottom in that toxic relationship to finally realize: *This is not worth it. I have to learn to love myself.*

I felt like I had failed, but the passage of time showed me it wasn't because my love hadn't fixed *him*. I had failed in fixing *myself*.

I thought it was an external failure, but in fact, it was an internal one. It takes courage to admit and make the necessary changes after we hold ourselves accountable for the part we played in tolerating mistreatment. It was hard for me coming out of that place, but I did it. And you can, too.

We have to believe that we are worthy of a love that empowers and appreciates us, and you need to be ready to invite this into your life when it arrives on your path.

Make the choice today to let go of those who bring you down. When you focus on strengthening your self-love, it sets a new standard for the love that you accept from others. Why would you tolerate less?

You deserve to be in the presence of those who feel like sunlight.

We feed the ego monster

As I mentioned earlier, I took a long time to find my direction in life. I'd discovered the hard way that university wasn't for me, but neither was the nine-to-five. After leaving my prison job, I fell into yet another depression.

Everything I was investing my energy into was failing to resonate. Hindsight would later make it clear that this was the season of rebirth – these experiences were meant to be explored, to bring awareness to the path I was destined to walk. What's more, the company my mum had worked for – her only job since her arrival in the UK – was in danger of going into liquidation. For the first time in her life, Mum's employment was in jeopardy. I'll tell you about the incredible influence her boss had on me later. But this period was extremely unsettling.

I had already set up a Tumblr account in 2011. I'd been hugely inspired by a few songs on the Wiz Khalifa mixtape *Kush & Orange Juice*, and I decided to dedicate a blog to sourcing positive lyrics from hip-hop songs. I created picture quotes and posted them on an hourly basis on Tumblr. My page blew up, and after my first three days, I woke up to 12,000 followers.

Tumblr is known as a place to authentically connect with people. Metrics mean nothing. You're purely admired or judged by the content of your blog. It's the best platform to grow a community that you can have an authentic bond with. The popularity of my Tumblr gave me the idea to start an online store with the slogan *Cool Story, Bro* on T-shirts and jumpers. Within three weeks of setting everything up, I'd already made my mum's yearly salary in sales. Neither of us could believe it. It just exploded! I remember one night, I stacked up all the PayPal invoices I'd printed out for the day and the pile was taller than my can of Red Bull.

I was making lots of money and building thousands of followers by the day. I was becoming what many people would perceive as a 'success.' But instead of making me happy and contented, it just fed into my insecure ego, and I became extremely conceited.

When ego takes over

This manifested in terrible ways. I became judgmental and almost resentful toward those whose lifestyles reflected the space I'd just escaped from. Like, *why are you slaving away for 'the man,' when you could be working for yourself?* I started to see people as lazy for not following the same path as me.

My empathy diminished by the day. I no longer allowed space for gray areas in my life. Everything became black or white. I was exposed to a different world. I began to network, and my access to people from different circles began to influence me negatively. I started to compare and second-guess my long-term friendships. Even my mum noticed the shift in my behavior and would often remind me of where I came from. But being humble wasn't an option. I was making money and my old life no longer resonated with me. Suffering was no longer my portion, and I refused to associate with anything that reminded me of it.

But under all this was a deep insecurity that convinced me that all this 'stuff' was necessary. My ego had taken over – it became one of my biggest distractions and it was turning me into a fool. And it took a massive shock to the system for me to reset my life and re-prioritize.

My mum was diagnosed with stage two breast cancer in 2013 and this revelation, almost immediately, changed my life. Two years prior, Mum's mother, my grandmother, and my aunt both passed away from cancer, so I knew how important it was for me not only to be present but to intentionally commit to her recovery.

I decided to stop blogging and devote myself to her as a full-time carer. Mum begged me to continue with my work, but I didn't want to – it was an honor to look after her, and we had more than enough money to survive.

The process of looking after Mum through her cancer treatment – a double mastectomy and chemo – was hard but was also a complete reset for both of us. For Mum, this was the first time she'd been unwell, and it brought her attention to the fragility of life. She immediately began to reassess her commitments to the things that weren't serving her. I found a sense of purpose in trying to restore my mum's health, and began looking further into alternative treatments and holistic approaches to health.

Mum's post-operative recovery journey made me value kindness more. I realized firsthand how impactful the kindness of others had been on our daily lives and also how destabilizing one word spoken carelessly could feel. So, I started to change the way I treated people and began to live with more intention.

Although I've had plenty of bumps in the road since then, this experience – which felt a bit like a psychological death and rebirth – showed me that living a life where I was just non-stop feeding my ego was just non-stop feeding my fear.

> Do you feel that you need to 'prove' yourself through external achievements, whether by earning lots of money, portraying a certain image, or having lots of followers on social media?

I see people living an ego-driven existence everywhere I turn. I see it with people who brag and overvalue themselves, treating others as if they are less-than. I can recognize it because that was me once, too – believing that the stuff you own, what you look like, and how others perceive you is what makes you a valuable person. But it all stems from the fact that you're not comfortable with yourself.

Don't blame yourself if you feel that ego is running your life, or you're constantly fueling the monster of insecurity by comparing yourself negatively with others. Our capitalist society feeds our ego by feeding us distractions. The more we spend our time and money on these distractions – on Netflix, alcohol, drugs, clothes, whatever it is – the more we invest value in meaningless things at the expense of our true selves.

It's only when we remove these distractions and let go of ego – let go of this superficial sense of self-importance – that we discover who we truly are.

Think about it: When people go on detoxes or retreats to reconnect with their souls and their purpose, they let go of all material distractions to do so. Nobody can do this sort of deep work if they're busy checking their DMs or responding to every message that comes through. Because if we're constantly distracted, ego wins.

And how many times have we believed that certain famous people or influencers are 'living their best life,' only to be shocked when they reveal they're depressed, or struggling with addiction? We might be like, *No, really? Them?* But in fact, we're only perceiving what their ego has chosen to show us, not their authentic truth.

Don't fake it

I have a split opinion on the concept of 'faking it until you make it.' Yes, it can be a stepping stone to discovering your strength and capabilities, like wearing a coat of confidence, but one that you're still growing into.

However, it's essential to remember that this coat is not a permanent outfit. While it's true that this concept of 'faking' can be useful in certain situations, it's still important to approach it with balance and self-awareness.

Faking it is mostly effective in situations where confidence and competence are needed to open doors to new opportunities. For example, as an influencer, a measure of confidence, even a small amount, is really important at the start of your journey. And even if it's not fully developed, this perceived confidence helps build trust with your audience and influences how they react to what you share.

However, it's also important to understand your limitations. Honesty and authenticity are valuable, and choosing to 'fake it' without the proper intentions can severely damage your credibility and relationships.

'Faking it' is designed to be a temporary strategy and should be coupled with a commitment to growth and learning. Remember the more you fake it, the further away you travel from your real self. Sooner or later, you have to face the truth about who you are as a person, and do you know what? Sometimes our truths are not pretty. But that's OK.

When you let go of ego and break yourself down, you can build yourself back up again.

We can all learn to detach ourselves from ego by inviting solitude and quiet into our lives. I'll explain in Part 2 how living intentionally and being alone can help us, but removing ourselves from distractions for a short while is a helpful first step. So, turn your phone off for an hour, or simply change a daily habit, like making sure it's not the first thing you reach for when you wake up.

Embrace solitude, reestablish a better relationship with your subconscious, and learn to fall in love with the magic that's developing within.

Ego is simply a mask for fear. What I've learned, though, is not to pretend it doesn't exist. I use it as a guide to ensure that I'm listening to my spirit. If I'm distracted by endlessly scrolling through meaningless content online, I can pause and take a step back. I can check in with what my spirit is really telling me – what am I avoiding? What is my ego preventing me from doing?

Reflection

I'm now back living in the flat I grew up in. It's humbling. I've made a lot of money and spent a lot of money. I've lived in luxury apartments and big villas, and now I'm grounded back in the place I started from. I learned to stop being a conceited idiot and face who I am. We can all do this; we just need to recognize what allowing our ego to dominate is doing to us – breaking our hearts.

As we move into how we start to heal our hearts, I want you to take a moment to reflect. Think about the things you may have done, the toxic relationships you may have invited in, the patterns you may have unintentionally created in your life that all contribute to the cycle of unhealthy habits that harm you.

If you haven't done so already, ask yourself:

- Do I depend on the validation of others to create my own happiness or self-worth?

- Have I held myself back because I'm not 'perfect' enough?

- Do I allow others' visions to dictate my life's path?

- Has my fear of the unknown kept me trapped in my comfort zone?

- Have I strayed so far from myself that I no longer recognize the person I am?

- Do I use my anger at others' failings as a mask for my own?

- Am I investing my time and energy into people who don't give back?

- Is my ego controlling me through constant distractions and feeding my insecurity?

We shouldn't feel shame if we answer 'yes' to any or all of these questions – hoarding feelings of guilt for the time we wasted won't erase the past. We can practice self-forgiveness, which is an amazing tool to have. It allows us to examine the past objectively so that we can make better choices moving forward. Let's give ourselves grace and hold ourselves accountable for the future – to use the wisdom we've obtained in a constructive way. That's where our power lies – in honesty and accountability. Let's move forward.

2 how we start to heal our hearts

The second part of this book is all about beginning to repair ourselves and our hearts. To help you with this, at the end of each chapter, I'll give you three things you can take into your life if the chapter resonates with you and what you're dealing with. Each of these are small but important steps to take, because they incorporate the three different facets of how we live our lives: in our thoughts, in what we say, and in our actions.

So, at the end of each chapter, you'll find short paragraphs encouraging you to Think, Ask, and Do. They're simply short suggestions on how to reframe your internal dialogue around the issue at hand, question(s) to ask yourself, and practical actions to take to progress to a better, healthier place in your life. Each chapter title is the piece of wisdom that I would love you all to hold in your heart as you begin the healing process.

We remember the most important relationship is with ourselves

When my mum was 60 years old, she finally put her relationship with herself first, and it was beautiful to see.

As you know from Part 1, Mum grew up in an abusive family. After having me, she made a vow to never expose me to the things she witnessed growing up in that house. She was determined to protect me from the same fate, but this didn't extend to her protecting herself. Her family consistently broke her heart throughout her adult life by lying to her face, being cruel, and constantly letting her down. She had great friends around her, who treated her with love and compassion, but she didn't receive the same from her family members – or even expect it from them. Once I was old enough to understand the negative impact this was having on her, I'd tell her to stop, to break off contact with them. I was confused as to why she kept going back into these toxic situations, but I underestimated the weight of guilt and loyalty she carried for them. She'd say over and over, 'Meggan, it's my family. What can I do?'

Mum started to have therapy on and off, and during those therapeutic periods she would improve. She would eat better and speak honestly with me about her feelings and her relationships with her family. She would apologize for certain behaviors that stemmed from this, and I would understand and support her as best I could. For a while, things would be good, and I'd hope this was the start of better times for her. But then her family would manipulate her back into the fold and things would change for the worse again. They'd start to attack her and let her down, and she would blame herself for allowing herself to be let down. She'd emotionally eat, put on weight, and suffer with low moods.

It was a self-fulfilling cycle of destruction.

When Mum was about to turn 60, I sat her down and asked her what she wanted for her birthday. It was a significant milestone, so I wanted to make it memorable. 'Oh, something small because you're already taking me home (to Trinidad), so I'm OK.' It was typical of Mum; she was always concerned about me saving my money, so I didn't think anything of it. But a bit later that night, she came into my room, sat on my bed, and held my hand. 'I'm going to be 60 years old, and over the last few weeks, I've been ruminating over why this is so significant for me,' she told me. 'Time is moving, girl. And I've wasted so many of my good years trying to preserve something that never existed. All I wanted was a family; even at 60, I miss Mother so much.'

Mother was my mum's grandmother, who raised her in Trinidad. I remember this conversation because her delivery was scattered, which was never like her. I knew she had come to an epiphany. 'What do you mean, Mum?' I asked her.

'Girl, you don't need to give me anything for my birthday because I'm giving it to myself. I'm giving myself back my life and my time. I'm going to promise to put myself first now. I'm letting them go for good,' she said.

In that moment, the world seemed to pause. Tears ran down my face as I sat, overwhelmed by the gravity of her words – it was the first time she'd ever chosen herself. And of course, putting it into practice was far from easy. She reached out to her siblings with a letter, a delicate and honest declaration of stepping back for her own well-being. The response? A cold 'LOL' from her younger sister, and no acknowledgment from the rest of her siblings. Cruel, right? But expected. It was a jarring reminder of the pain a narcissist can inflict; they'll do anything to break you down and pull you back into their chaos.

Despite my deepest fears, Mum remained true to her promise. She spent the next few years gently turning the pages of her new life into chapters that she wrote for herself. Putting her needs first. Not that this involved anything flashy or dramatic.

She led a humble life and kept a simple routine. By this time, she had retired from work, so she could shape her weeks however she liked. 'On Monday, I'll go to Sainsbury's; on Wednesday, I'll do yoga,' she'd share, finding joy in the simple things. It was all everyday stuff. But the difference was she began to embrace her essence and became unapologetically herself again. With a smile on my face, I would playfully call her a 'neek' (which is slang for geek): It was like her inner child had finally come out to play. It was amazing to see, but I only wish she'd done it earlier, so she could have had more time to enjoy her life to the full.

Learning to see that self-love isn't selfish

The transformation in my mum was huge. She finally began to recognize her own worth and value. She learned that prioritizing herself wasn't an act of selfishness, but instead, a deep form of self-love, a lesson I believe we could all benefit from. A truth that, in time, became a lesson that I learned for myself, too.

You've probably guessed by now that I spent a great deal of my life being a people pleaser, always putting others first. My own experiences mirrored what I saw my mum do – a testament to how our upbringing molds us. I would put myself second and disregard the importance of maintaining my own plans. I always focused my time on helping others strengthen their foundations and build a beautiful, strong house; meanwhile, I left my own house neglected, falling apart, and covered in weeds.

No one reciprocated my level of exertion. I'd always go the extra mile, but it seemed like no one was willing to walk with me. It became clear that my efforts for others had set an expectation that I couldn't sustain. I realized something was seriously wrong. By not setting the proper boundaries, and through my reluctance to change, I passively gave people the permission to undervalue me. I would feel a deep sense of betrayal at those times when I would make myself readily available but my needs weren't met with the same level of urgency. However, in those moments of reflection, I recognized my part in this and realized I only had myself to blame.

We teach others how to treat us by what we allow. How could I blame others for feeling entitled to my time, when my own behavior consistently signaled that they were more important to me than myself?

My deficiency in self-love and my inability to assert my boundaries were beginning to take a toll on me. I yearned to give myself the same energy that I was distributing outward. I wanted to be on the receiving end of my benevolence, to experience firsthand what it felt like to be loved by me.

Setting boundaries and building better relationships

The first step I took toward developing a stronger sense of self-love was establishing my boundaries with others. For me, that meant no longer being easily accessible, even to the extent of turning off my WhatsApp notifications so I didn't feel compelled to respond immediately. I also learned how to adopt a healthier relationship with my time, so I no longer found it sustainable to devote the hours that I should be utilizing for my own journey into accompanying others with theirs. I came to understand that being kind to others isn't synonymous with sacrificing my peace – a lesson I struggled with at first, and which also came with a side serving of guilt.

Setting boundaries is rarely a straightforward process – usually because it involves shifting the behavior of those around us who've become accustomed to our old ways. The sudden changes don't always deliver well either, and sometimes it results in being perceived or labeled as being a 'problem.' I can only imagine how confusing it must have been for those who were used to my people-pleasing ways. They must have thought, *What's going on? You were OK with this just the other day. What's changed?*

Remember, our boundaries are designed to protect us from the external harm that seeks to deplete us; they are not an attack on the other person.

However, others might not see it that way. When you decide to reclaim your time, the people who've had infinite access to you will feel like you're stealing from them. They may feel slighted, simply because your behavior has shifted from what they've been used to. (And as we've explored already, change can be challenging for us all.) The most effective way to implement these boundaries is to be clear and transparent – tell people what is changing and why. I'll go into more detail about boundaries in Part 3, too, as they're so important.

Of course, there will be times when people flat-out disregard our boundaries, regardless of how clearly we communicate them. It's important to recognize when it's time to take a step back, when to protect your energy, or when to walk away, rather than serving as an endless resource for those who feel entitled to you. If there are people in your life who continually and nonchalantly cross your boundaries, it's essential to limit their access to you. You can always adjust your life around their absence. It's important to remember that you're not bound to anyone. You always have the right to leave.

What self-love is, and what it isn't

In the same way that 'authenticity' can be misunderstood (which I touched upon in Part 1), I want to be abundantly clear about the differences between self-love and the lack of it. Self-love isn't an

When you decide to reclaim your time, the people who've had infinite access to you will feel like you're stealing from them.

excuse to do whatever we want, at any given time. That's not how this works – plus, we probably wouldn't be so appealing to others if we acted like that. We all have different obligations in life. However, we owe it to those who genuinely love us to give them the opportunity to witness what it looks like when we finally redirect the love that we freely distribute to others *back to ourselves*. Because, after all, what we nurture within radiates into our external world.

Dedicating ourselves to practices that cultivate self-love is the cornerstone of sustaining healthier relationships. These may include honoring your inner peace by implementing new mindful ways of raising your vibrations, bringing calm back into your vicinity, or accepting your beauty as it stands – realizing that you're simply a combination of those who came before you and the same features you pick apart and compare are most likely attached to the stories of survival that made it possible for you to be here today.

When we nurture our love within, we lay the foundations for the new connections that we're welcoming in. The most encouraging thing you could ever showcase is a deep appreciation for yourself. By strengthening our self-love, we get to create a new standard for the treatment we're willing to accept from others.

Because why would we settle for less than what we can graciously provide for ourselves?

Think

Self-love isn't selfish. When you cultivate love and respect for yourself, the people in your life will treat you accordingly, because you're leading by example.

Ask

Are there people in your life who take more than they give? Do you equate your worth as a good friend, child, or partner with your constant availability, neglecting your own needs in the process? How is this truly affecting you emotionally?

Do

Reserve a two-hour slot in your calendar each week and dedicate it solely to you. Distribute this time however best it serves you, whether that's weekly, biweekly, or even half an hour each day – whatever works.

Turn off your phone, breathe deeply, and fully engage with yourself. It could be journaling (written or vocal), going for a walk in nature, hitting the gym, meditating (whether in silence or through sound healing, like singing bowls), taking a long bath with the correct essential oils and salts to match the energy you're trying to download, or reading a good book.

Allow no distractions or interruptions – if you live with others, inform them that this time is crucial, so they can respect your need for uninterrupted space.

We start over whenever we need to

Where did we all get the idea that we only get one chance to start again in our lives?

I think we've all been influenced by the narratives we see in the movies. The hero or heroine faces a crisis, hits rock bottom, and then bounces back and everything miraculously improves. It's promoted as a linear journey; they fall, they learn, they succeed, and then **boom**, all is done, dusted, and neatly wrapped up in a two-hour time frame.

The only trouble is – it's nonsense. Yes, movies have a limited running time, but the truth remains. Problems are trivialized and reduced to easy fixes that ridicule our reality, resulting in the viewer adopting a wave of unrealistic expectations regarding time. Life is messy. Problems can take months – sometimes years – to resolve, and that's fine. But to expect life to naturally fall into place is a dangerous delusion to live by. The reality is that life consists of a variation of highs and lows. We have the chance to reset and start anew, as many times as we need to. I've done this countless times.

Life is full of challenges

If I tried to measure the ups and downs in my life, that graph would be anything but a straight line. In fact, it would be a haphazard, manic scrabble, that would probably result in you looking at me sideways and asking if everything is OK at home. But this is simply because my journey with growth has led me down some unfathomable paths, and I've come to accept that this is completely fine. I often wonder if life is a series of opportunities, guiding us closer toward our higher selves, and the only way we hinder this journey is by choosing to disengage from our evolution, by resisting growth.

Take the chakras, for example. Every chakra symbolizes a new level of elevation that is separated by a seven-year cycle. There are seven main chakras, which means we only truly become fully developed conscious beings at the age of 49. At 49, it's believed that we've encountered everything that life had in store for our paths, and if we acted accordingly, this would transform us into our highest evolved state. For me, that proves that life is destined to come attached with a series of challenges and it's something that we cannot avoid happening. We can decide to ignore these callings, and thus stifle our personal growth, but that's a frightening existence to strive for.

I didn't emerge as a new person after my first crisis and, even now, I wouldn't be so quick to say, 'I'm fixed.' But I do carry a wealth of wisdom with me, and I'm more than happy to embrace this new perspective that causes young people to label me as 'Auntie.'

The truth is, I used to be petrified of starting anew. My first major setback, when my friend Kyle passed away, was such a frightening time. I felt so bleak. The brightness of life dulled before me, and it took years for life's colors to return to their original hues. I hit another low during college, where I felt utterly lost and anxious about my future. Dropping out of university caused me to endure another depression. And in my early 20s, societal pressures led me to believe that it was 'too late' for me to succeed. I could go on…

I know now that those fears were baseless, but it didn't feel that way at the time. It was a desperate period for me. I'd convinced myself that I'd failed just because I didn't follow the hand-me-down script that was given to me by my mum and my community. Eventually, I realized that when it comes to the trajectory of your life, if you fail to make a decision on the path you want to take, eventually that decision will be made for you.

Even when I achieved material success through my social media ventures, I was still grappling with a profound inner struggle. I became so consumed with entrepreneurship that my life began to narrow down to the glow of a computer screen. Nothing else occupied me. Friends and family gradually faded into the background, and my existence started to feel automated and empty. The lifestyle I'd created became unsustainable and impacted my overall psychological health. I found myself in a loop of lingering low moods and overall unhappiness.

To be completely transparent, what held me back was a lack of self-belief. I was crippled by the fear of being visible and refused to take risks, which left me in a state of stagnancy. Over time, fatigue set in. I grew increasingly tired of who I was becoming. Tired of not having the confidence to live in my truth, tired of fearing my potential, tired of living on the sidelines while watching everyone around me thrive, tired of waking up consumed with sorrow, tired of disappointing the people who were rooting for me, tired of Mum asking me when I was going to step into my purpose, and tired of the 'what ifs,' 'buts,' and 'maybes' that I used as a shield against trying again.

Finding strength when we fail

My point is, I came to realize that the path I was on wasn't meant for me, and it took many more tries to truly understand that. I have picked myself back up again countless times in my life, even as recently as 2021, when I found myself completely alone. (I share this story properly on page 111.) I accept that I might need to start over again at another point in the future. Who knows? Life is full of challenges, unexpected crises we haven't planned for, and periods where we'll feel stuck – and that's all right.

The most important thing is not that these difficult times happen – after all, they're inevitable – but that we find the strength to get back up again after we fall.

In many ways, I believe that social media often perpetuates the myth that our lives should be flawlessly mapped out, without any setbacks. Like I've said, we're only shown the highlights others choose to display, which leads to the false perception that others don't fail like we do, or they don't face any struggles, or that they've made the right decisions for themselves once, in one go, and now everything has seamlessly fallen into place. But that's far from the truth. The reality is nobody has it all figured out. Nobody.

Learning to move forward more than once

If you find yourself at a low point, one you've visited before, don't fall into the trap of believing you've exhausted your chances of starting over. It's not true. (And guess what? No one is keeping score, either.) Instead, what we can do is support ourselves in moving forward, free from self-criticism and judgment. We just need to be consciously aware of what's happening and extend kindness to ourselves, acknowledging that fear is often the only thing standing in the way of us starting over again.

Yes, fear again! We're so terrified of failure that we resist trying again. We spend too much time worrying about our capabilities and the potential judgments of others, obsessing over what people will think about us if we don't succeed this time. We find ourselves caught in a loop of doubts. *Can I really do this? Is this too big for me? What will people say if I don't do it? Or worse, what if I go through with it and fail?*

I believe there's something really liberating in acknowledging this: People will always have their opinions, and there's absolutely nothing we can do to control that. Isn't that great? Isn't that a relief? It may not feel like it (believe me, as someone who once thrived on pleasing others, I would *not* have wanted to hear this a few years ago), but it's true.

The only opinions and expectations that truly count are the ones we hold about ourselves. Falling short of our own standards is the real issue, not other people's opinions.

There's nothing worse than knowing you're not aligned with your true purpose. During the struggles I shared earlier, I did everything I could to avoid my inner voice, busying myself to distract myself from having to address the inner war that was bubbling within. For a long time, it seemed easier to get lost in the noise. However, everything shifted for me when I chose to confront myself, take risks, and truly engage with life. You can do the same, no matter how many attempts you make. You cannot avoid yourself, and you cannot avoid failure. So, take it off your list of worries.

All of us will fail at some point in our lives – probably more than once. What truly matters is how we respond to these failures. That's all.

Think

Remember that we're under no obligation to have it all together all the time. Nobody made that rule up, so give yourself a break.

Ask

What if you fail this time around? Really, what is the worst that can happen if you do? Will the world truly end? Are you afraid of the actual act of failure and how that might make you feel? Or is it the perception of failure that is holding you back?

Do

Read books and quotes of people who celebrate repeated failures. There's a great quote from Michael Jordan, the basketball superstar, where he says: 'I missed more than 9,000 shots in my career. I've lost almost 300 games. Twenty-six times I've been trusted to take the game-winning shot – and missed. I've failed over and over and over again in my life. And that is why I succeed.'

We say 'yes' to new experiences

When I was 10, a new chapter unfolded, and my life opened up for the first time. It was during the summer holidays, and I was restless with boredom.

My mum gave me an allowance of £2.50 per day, along with the challenge of stretching it to cover both necessities and fun while I was with the childminder. This budget was modest compared to my friends' allowances and unlike them, my household chores didn't translate to extra cash. I grew agitated trying to find ways of making money and one day, I brought my concerns to my mum. 'Mum, this money – it's not enough. I have plans and this is slowing me down.'

Her response came with a smile. 'OK, get ready for 8 a.m. tomorrow, and we'll see what Thomas has to say,' she said, when I suggested pitching my services at her workplace. I'm not exaggerating when I say the lessons I learned from my mum's boss completely changed my life in so many ways.

Gaining opportunities to grow and learn

Thomas Glaser's name has been a constant in my mother's narrative since her teenage years, shortly after she arrived in England. He inherited his family's business – a clothing brand that catered to older women – and his clothes featured in boutiques across London and countrywide. It was more than a business; it was a family – to which he welcomed my mother warmly.

Starting as a fabric cutter, her grit and commitment to learning saw her rise to the role of bookkeeper. Thomas and my mum had a great working relationship, and she even looked after his children on occasions when he would take his wife out for the evening. And in my earliest days, when a babysitter was out of reach, he welcomed me into the office with open arms. When Thomas passed away, Mum was left to close the business, something she did with honor. Glaser's was her first and only job. She worked there for 40 years.

At a young age, Thomas introduced me to a raft of opportunities that were worlds apart from anything school offered me. Once he saw my work ethic and dedication to learning, he offered me £50 a week to sort invoices and pick out garments in preparation for shipping. This was the most money I'd ever seen in my life. I remember thinking, *Fifty quid a week? Yo, I'm going to be rich!* Even Mum thought it was steep.

Before I knew it, I was working a few hours per day, and as I took on more responsibilities, my wages grew to £250 a week. Cash. He trusted me and that trust was an amazing feeling to have. I continued to work for him for years, even during school terms. I'd catch the W9 bus at half-past three, right after the school bell, to put in a few hours at his office. The pride of earning my keep fueled my drive to save every penny. My goal was clear: to buy my own car by the age of 17.

Opening my eyes to a new world

Thomas reiterated the importance of delayed gratification, a concept my mum had always emphasized, especially when I started receiving pocket money. But Thomas's entire life was a manifestation of that. His lifestyle, presumably a result of his success as a company director, was something I'd never encountered before. This experience opened the doors to a completely new world from the one I'd been brought up in. His granddaughter, who occasionally visited him at work, became a friend of mine. She invited me over to their house one day to go for a swim. I was so naive back then; I didn't even realize people could have swimming pools at their house!

Visiting their home was an awakening. The sheer size of their lobby, compared to the downstairs of my entire home, was difficult to grasp. It was huge! The swimming pool alone left me in awe, and they even had tennis courts and a view overlooking a golf course. It was a completely different environment to anything I had ever experienced – a glimpse into another world. Of course, to his granddaughter, this was normal, so I didn't say anything at the time. Despite the crisp weather and the leaf-filled pool, as we dove into the water together, all I could think was how amazing this whole experience was.

That evening, when I got home, I was still trying to make sense of everything. I walked to the back door led to our garden, stared at my swing, and I asked my mum, 'How come Thomas's house is so big compared to ours?'

I shared how impressed I was with his place, and her response was simple, yet profound: 'This is what I wanted you to see – it's the difference between working for somebody and working for yourself.' That night, I vowed never to work for anyone else. Of course, I did end up having a few odd jobs here and there, but it never felt right. Thomas had opened my eyes to the possibility of building your own life based on a passion – a lesson that has stayed with me and fueled the success of The Good Quote.

Thomas's trust in me instilled a level of confidence I'd never had before that point. It wasn't just about managing files; it was about the financial responsibility, too. It was my job to take the earnings from the company to the bank. He'd pass me a massive envelope with loads of money in it, which I had to take to the counter – I know it seems crazy, because I was just a kid, but this task taught me to communicate confidently with adults, and that if I was trustworthy, I would be rewarded. I respected and admired him so much and when I told him, 'I want to be just like you when I grow up,' he smiled and reiterated that that was the reason why he was investing in me. The lessons I learned from him, simply by being in his presence, were invaluable.

Learning lifelong lessons from saying 'yes'

I'm sharing this story because all these amazing teachings came out of saying 'yes' to a new experience. Even though I was so young when I first started working for Mr. Glaser, it opened a window to a world that I couldn't have found on my own. It showed me that observing other people's lives is an incredible way to broaden your own horizons. I took that with me throughout my life, and it has held me in such good stead. Even through my periods of depression and self-sabotage, I've been able to remember all the good that comes out of saying 'yes.'

By embracing new experiences – even when our first instinct might be to shy away – we are nourishing our souls.

This might sound a little hippyish, but I believe our soul's desire is to explore the possibilities of its potential. When we hesitate, stagnate, cling to our 'discomfort' zones, and allow fear and doubt to dominate, we suppress that potential. This isn't about ignoring our gut feelings – far from it, and I plan to delve more into the topic of our intuition soon. It's about not allowing our worst habits to hold us back by preventing us from experimenting with something new.

Life often presents us with situations that are unfamiliar and, understandably, it can be scary to say 'yes.' But when we put barriers up to new experiences, we deaden our hearts. The comfort of saying 'no,' especially out of fear of failure or the unknown, is all too tempting. My advice? The next time you find yourself in a situation where you have to say 'yes' or 'no,' pause. Think: *Why am I going to answer the way I am?* Really reflect deeply about it. Of course, I'm not telling you to never say 'no' to anything! There are loads of times when we can use 'no' as the most powerful word in our arsenal (much like when I talked about setting boundaries earlier). But when faced with a genuine opportunity, one that isn't harmful, risky, or draining to our well-being, consider the possibilities that saying 'yes' might unfold, and what you might miss by choosing 'no.'

Remember, everything we do now, we once did for the first time. Simple things like brushing our teeth or writing our name were new to us once. As children, we embraced these tasks, and if we didn't, our parents made us. This willingness to try new things is how we learned. But I've noticed the older we grow, the more reluctant we become to say 'yes' to experiences that could further improve our lives. It's as if the comfort of the reality we've built for ourselves makes the uncertainty of saying 'yes' intimidating. We even celebrate and feel a sense of excitement when we finally say 'yes' after some sort of hesitation.

When I was younger, I made a promise to myself not to let adulthood make me forget the essence that makes life worth living. We must continue to embrace 'yes,' seeking out new opportunities that come our way, or that we can invite in through positive affirmations. It's about keeping that childlike openness alive!

Think

What we experience today will be lessons for us to learn tomorrow. Without new experiences, we'll never learn anything new.

Ask

What are the qualities of the person you most admire in your life? Are they open, or closed off? Courageous or timid? Interested or dismissive? Have they said 'yes' to new avenues in their life?

Do

Think about a time in your life when you welcomed in a new experience. It can be anything, big or small, and it might even have been something another person persuaded you to do, even if you felt reluctant at first! Now, thinking about this new experience, write down your answers to these questions:

- What were your fears or worries before this new experience?

- Did these fears manifest? Or did you discover that they disappeared?

- If the fears did manifest, how did you deal with them?

- How did you feel after this new experience?

We embrace solitude as a way to get to know ourselves again

I thought I understood what it meant to be alone, but I didn't, until my mum passed away.

Many years ago, a conversation with a friend led me to start appreciating the value of solitude. Back then, in my early 20s, my life was in complete disarray. This was the period when I saw my peers thriving, their futures mapped out, moving forward with what I perceived to be purposeful direction. I, on the other hand, was an unemployed university dropout, struggling to find my feet and often feeling hopeless about my future. I kept myself busy by engaging in various forms of distraction, not brave enough to face myself and my issues. There were moments when I felt like giving up entirely.

'How much time do you *actually* spend by yourself?' asked my friend, whom I was venting to about my inability to manage my time correctly and how much I was craving solitude. I thought I knew the answer.

'Whenever I'm alone, I'm spending time with myself, right?'

But as we listed out my typical activities during 'me time,' it quickly became evident that even in solitude, I was never *truly* alone with myself. I was constantly flirting with escapism – endless scrolling through social media, Netflix binges, or long drives with no destination. I was doing anything I possibly could to distract myself, and therefore prolonging the act of self-confrontation, which inadvertently stunted my growth and created a sense of stagnation and frustration.

Through making changes in my life, I learned that true stillness and solitude are the main components needed to explore the depths of our being. When we practice turning inward, we become aware of the whispers within. This was something I drew on when I had to face the lowest, hardest point of my life.

Facing the worst trauma of my life

In 2020, my deepest fear became a reality: Mum's cancer returned. This time, it was more aggressive and invaded her bones, the circumference of her skull, and her neck. God, it was so hard to see my mum go through such physical, emotional, and mental pain. I got through it by reminding myself I had a job to do, which was to do anything I could to prolong her life. Mum was my everything. It had been me and her forever. We traveled to Saint Lucia during the Covid-19 pandemic, and although my life of extravagance had always been too much for my mum – she was a small, humble lady – I spent as much money as I could on natural remedies in a bid to help her, along with private medical experts, scans, and nursing care.

Despite all these efforts, it was too late. She passed away in March 2021. It was the most traumatic experience of my life. I couldn't fathom that my mum was gone. The day she died, and the days that followed, were a blurred haze of numbness. There were moments when I wasn't even sure that I wanted to go on. I went through the most horrendous weeks of chaos, shock, and grief as I navigated the complex process of arranging her funeral over in Trinidad, honoring her last wishes to rest there.

For the first time in my life, I found myself completely alone, and I had to learn to stand on my own two feet. It was far from easy – what I went through after my mum passed could make an entire book in itself. But I had to go through the pain of losing my mum on my own, because it was my personal pain to go through. Through my previous experiences with stagnation and depression, I'd learned that everything we run away from still resides within us, so our pain will always trail behind us, no matter how far we stray or what we try to do.

We can never escape ourselves and our emotions, and we have an innate responsibility to establish a healthy relationship with ourselves (which is what this book is really all about). This is why we need to do the work and face ourselves – not only to ensure we develop true self-awareness but also to build the inner strength we need when life throws these immense challenges our way. So, when grief took me over, I had to sit with it and go through the worst of it, because it was completely unavoidable.

I understand how difficult it can be for some of us to be alone – for many, it feels almost painful to not have people around. This can be for all sorts of different reasons; some struggle to be in their own company because the silence can amplify the thoughts they're trying to avoid; others might be naturally extroverted, which means

True stillness and solitude
are the main components
needed to explore the
depths of our being. When
we practice turning inward,
we become aware of the
whispers within.

they gain their personal energy from communicating and engaging with others. But neither of these reasons, nor any other, is a reason to avoid solitude.

The strength of intentional solitude

Integrating solitude into our lives is not just beneficial, but essential. There's a significant difference between solitude and loneliness. Solitude is intentional. It's a choice; loneliness is not.

Solitude offers a sense of beauty, allowing us to exist without superficial distractions and delve deeper into self-discovery.

In Part 1, I explored how feeding our ego only nourishes our insecurities. Learning to embrace solitude is essentially the antithesis of that. It encourages us to release our fixation on superficial self-importance and instead, become comfortable adopting true self-awareness and being our own best friend. This is why many who practice meditation, including Buddhists and spiritual leaders, regard solitude as a central part of their lives – it's a pathway to understanding and inner peace.

I know it's not something that everybody is able to do, but solitude retreats, when feasible, can be incredibly rewarding. Even if it's just a quiet corner at home, carving a space for self-reflection can be an amazing route into self-knowledge. If we're constantly distracted or disproportionately focused on spending our time and energy on external matters, when will we find the time to strengthen, evolve, and nourish a relationship within? (If this isn't feasible, don't worry; there are other options. I've given additional suggestions below.)

Understanding ourselves is a challenging journey, and it's not about patting ourselves on the back all the time. Like I've said, sometimes facing our truths can be unsettling. But through intentional solitude and spending time *truly* alone with our thoughts, we can develop clarity. For me, embracing solitude in the aftermath of my mum's passing meant confronting my grief head-on and living side by side with my pain. It was about learning to accept the days where I woke up and my heart was still broken. But I learned to trust the unfolding process, getting through it, moment by moment.

Think

In this hyper-connected world, where we're judged by the number of followers we have on social media, it's easy to devalue solitude. Choosing solitude is a power, not a weakness.

Ask

How does the idea of being alone make you feel? If you feel uncomfortable, why is that? What emotions does it spark? If you feel good at the idea of solitude, what does that feel like?

Do

Start to spend some time when you are truly alone – and that means no phones, even on silent! Start with just 10 minutes daily in a quiet place, when you know nobody will interrupt you. Gradually, as you make this a regular practice, see if you can build up the minutes.

There's no rush, and you don't need to put pressure on yourself to meditate or be 'mindful' for the longest time possible. It isn't a competition; there's no gold star. Just let the time unfold as it will.

We view asking for help as a superpower

For a long time, I'd held tightly onto the belief that asking for help was a weakness. This was something I was eventually forced to confront, and I've grown to learn that, in fact, the opposite is true.

I used to pride myself on being the person others could lean on, a sort of superhero, but I never extended that level of compassion to myself. Of course, I couldn't fathom the idea that there would ever be a time in my life when I would need help. *Why? I can handle my own scene by myself.* In my mind, 'help' was a one-way street. Yet, this perspective didn't serve me well – life has a way of humbling us. The people I attempted to help weren't fixed by my efforts. Instead, I was faced with resistance and a lack of cooperation. It's almost as if my mission to help others was purposely failing because I was interrupting their destiny while neglecting my own needs in the process. My preoccupation with others left me in a distracted state, straying further and further away from myself.

Reframing my attitude to assistance

I used to think that my resistance to seeking help was because I'd never needed it. I barely saw my mum receive help, either. She always had a solution, and it always went to plan. She was extremely independent and self-sustaining. But my case was different.

Throughout my life, I've been on the receiving end of a lot of constructive assistance. Starting, obviously, with my mum, the elders in my community, and teachers like Mr. P. – my head of year at secondary school, who met me halfway when I had a negative attitude toward learning. Lincoln Beckford, the mentor in our community who stepped in to mend our spirits when we lost Kyle. Thomas Glaser, my mum's boss, who helped me see a world beyond the confines of my immediate surroundings. My business partner, Wale Kalejaiye, who's supported me creatively throughout my entire entrepreneurial journey. Their help was generously given, and I was lucky to receive it.

As I embarked on my long period of self-betterment, my perspective on asking for help began to shift. I realized that it takes strength to ask for help, or to admit your vulnerabilities. Even so, the full weight of this truth didn't hit me until I lost my mum. I was completely defenseless. And it's only then that I really understood the true strength that comes from reaching out for help.

It's a powerful act to ask for a hand to hold, a shoulder of support, or a listening ear during your darkest hours. And it's in these moments of reaching out when we can truly witness the sincerest examples of connection and support.

Allowing others to help me during grief

My mum passed away in Saint Lucia, an island she always favored outside of Trinidad for its botanical beauty. It was during the Covid-19 pandemic, and we were stranded due to travel restrictions. I became disorientated and completely disconnected from myself. The weight of my grief while being stuck on an island consumed me.

The people from the local community (an extension of the friends we'd made) reached out and cared for me. Their kindness became my anchor. My mum's last wishes were to be returned to her grandmother, but I didn't have the finances to transport her vessel.

I begged my grandfather for help, and he covered the costs. After her funeral, I had to remain in Trinidad for a year, due to the closed borders, and I plunged into a deep depression.

Family who I thought I could depend on used this as an opportunity to chastise me. 'Finally, you're getting a taste of reality,' I was told. 'Your mum isn't here to save you. Where can your followers take you now?' In fact, the day of my mum's funeral, my cousin refused to let me bathe in the family bathroom – instead, I had to bathe outside with a hosepipe, where the dogs resided. Using the remainder of my savings, I left their property and rented a small apartment within the heart of the community, next to a so-called 'ghetto' in Marabella. There, I found myself surrounded by the kindest people I had ever met.

Their lives were a stark contrast to what we typically see in the UK. My mother was born and raised in a board house, with galvanized roofing and a latrine in the back. So, I was very much prepared for the realities of my situation, but living there day to day differed significantly from my previous annual visits. For the first time, I was faced with the harsh truths of what 'poverty-stricken' people truly go through.

A community that's often judged by the majority held stronger moral values than many people in more prestigious surroundings. I saw men up early in the morning, working government jobs, trying to make ends meet, and I saw women with many hustles, from cooking and cleaning to assembling furniture, reach the end of each week with enough money to support their families. Even the local drug-dependent people cleaned up the common areas in exchange for money for food. The hood had its own ecosystem. The only disadvantage was the violence that was perpetuated by internal politics.

Amid this, one woman's story left an indelible impression on me. She was a hustler, a local fisherwoman, with a strong work ethic and a stronger mind. She would ration funds, and work long hours in the ocean, just to provide her daughter with a better path. Naturally, this reminded me of how opportunities had flowed so seamlessly to me due to my mother's sacrifices and hard work. The fisherwoman had a deep spiritual practice and mentioned God in almost every sentence. She couldn't believe that I was born in 'foreign' from a woman who was raised in similar surroundings to hers. She told me it was dishonorable to my mother's memory to squander my days in sorrow.

I was entangled in a web of self-destructive behaviors – anything to blur the trauma I'd faced witnessing my mum pass away in such extreme circumstances. I would start and end my days smoking and drinking rum, and would casually google ways to ethically end my life, without making God angry. I was lost in a haze of depression.

Then came a day of reckoning, when the fisherwoman looked at me with complete conviction and said, 'Girl, nah you doh need to be here. I've been following your Instagram for years; you've got opportunities I couldn't even think of. Get up nahman!' It was a huge wake-up call. A reminder to reclaim the life my mum worked so hard to give me.

In seeking connection and support, I reached out across my network – colleagues, friends, and even casual acquaintances from Instagram. Piece by piece, I began reconstructing my life, not just by returning to work and regaining financial stability, but also by being transparent and vulnerable about how I was struggling to cope in the wake of my mum's passing. The depth of my grief was perplexing, and I was left with a tapestry of questions: *Why does it feel like I lost a child? Maybe because I was her carer? I know she's passed away, but I need to tell her about the things that have happened since she left. Why has the hue of colors around me dulled? Will I ever look at a sunset in the same way again? This is the longest I've gone without speaking to my mum, my best friend. Who do I confide in now? Why did Mum only see her worth and value in the last six years of her life? Why did this happen to us?*

Yeah… this journey was not without its challenges.

Help flows like waves, and when the tide is out, it's easy to persuade ourselves that it's out of reach. It leaves us feeling deserted, abandoned, and alone on the bare shore. But, as always, help returns, like waves of the incoming tide, brushing against our feet.

A friend of mine put me in touch with a therapist, who presented me with some truths that I was unprepared to accept. After our session, I didn't speak to him for a further nine months. I was too consumed in my destructive behavior and wasn't ready to heal or face my reality. Yet, even in my absence, my therapist, Michael Adams, didn't give up on me. He would check in sporadically, reassuring me *I'll be here for you when you're ready*. His patience was a gift, one that eventually helped me reach a place of acceptance and heal in unfathomable ways.

It's interesting who the universe sends to you, strangers who will leave permanent marks on your path in the future.

Understanding the power of asking for help

So many people have helped me in recent years. I used to think such 'good people' were nonexistent. I became so accustomed to the chaos I'd let into my life that the notion of peace brought by others seemed like a distant memory. My experiences taught me that help flows like waves, and when the tide is out, it's easy to persuade ourselves that it's out of reach. It leaves us feeling deserted, abandoned, and alone on the bare shore. But, as always, help returns, like waves of the incoming tide, brushing against our feet. And if we choose, we can step forward and meet it, and immerse ourselves in its grace once more.

I know I'm not alone when it comes to learning to ask for help and accepting it. Why do we find it so difficult to do? I believe there are many reasons behind this. From a tender age, we're taught that strength lies in self-reliance, that it's 'strong' to be independent, to fight your own battles, and that to 'grow up' means to become less dependent on others. What's more, this world can often feel like a lonely place, and the more digital our communications are, the wider the distance between us becomes. Sometimes it's easy to feel like society doesn't place much value on real connections anymore. A lot of relationships, especially online ones, have transactional undertones that leave us feeling empty. During Covid, this feeling only grew within us, as we couldn't connect physically.

Why accepting help is not dependency

We must learn that asking for help is not a sign of weakness, nor does it mean you're being dependent on others. In fact, they're completely different things. Asking someone for help is a courageous act: You're making yourself momentarily vulnerable with someone else, showing them you trust and value their support. Being overly dependent on others, as we've seen, is transferring your sense of self-worth onto another person. It's healthy to seek support, to reach out, but it's crucial to maintain our independence and not rely on others for our self-esteem. The former is a choice of strength, the latter a surrender of power.

It is a transformative change of perspective. Once we accept that no one owes us anything, we start to appreciate those who go out of their way for us even more. We're not entitled to a helping hand, but we are worthy of it. Learn to accept it when it arrives and ask for it when needed. Anything positive we receive from someone is a gift that must be appreciated.

Think

Asking for help is nothing to be ashamed of. You won't lose respect if you decide to let go and delegate to someone else. Teamwork only works if you let your team work.

Ask

When was the last time you asked somebody for help? Why did you do it then and what was the outcome? How did you feel afterward?

Do

Think of one thing, however small, that you are struggling to manage on your own. It can be anything, from putting a job application together or finding a holiday destination, to not having the right ingredients in the fridge! Then pluck up the courage and ask somebody you know well if they can help you out with this. Baby steps!

We forgive ourselves for settling for less than we deserve

Right now, I think it's fair to say that I'm in one of the most nurturing relationships I've ever experienced. And to be clear, I'm not saying this to boast. The truth is, it's taken me years of less-than-ideal relationships to arrive at this point. Only now can I fully grasp how unhealthy my past relationships truly were.

Honestly, when I look back and revisit some of the connections I fought so hard to maintain, I can't help but ask myself, *What on earth was I thinking?* Like, how many prayers will it take to remove these memories from my mind? I can't even fathom why I felt so comfortable being in those spaces in the first place. But the truth is, at the time, I was more than comfortable; these environments were my sanctuaries.

I no longer allow myself to dwell on past mistakes. I replace that energy with gratitude, and give thanks that those experiences, as harsh as they were, now provide clarity on the level of growth I have accumulated since then. One example was a guy I dated in my mid-20s. My friends practically pleaded with me to break it off. I was so lost at the time that I really couldn't see how bad he was for me.

Back then, I was riddled with insecurity, my self-esteem was in the gutter, and my confidence was virtually nonexistent. I was more focused on how great we looked together as a couple than protecting myself from the emotional strain that the relationship was having on me. I couldn't be myself – doing so only exacerbated the tensions in our relationship. For example, he once boasted that he found pleasure in embarrassing me in front of others. There was an instance where he was shopping for his first car. As I asked the salesman to show us the latest offers, suddenly the atmosphere changed. My ex threw a tantrum and walked out, leaving me and the salesman smiling awkwardly at each other as I picked up my belongings and hastily followed my ex out. Apparently, I'd been too friendly. Other times, he would create moments where I would feel safe enough to share my deepest insecurities with him, only for him to take that information and use it as ammunition in our future arguments.

By the end of this relationship, I had gained over 55lb (25kg). Fifty-five pounds of added stress that was scattered all over my body. I was in a terrible state, physically and emotionally. My mum tried to convince me I deserved better, but I just couldn't see it. Now, when I look back at photos from that period, I see myself through a whole new lens, completely different from how I felt about myself at the time.

Gaining perspective about damaging relationships

As I mentioned earlier, I believe our energy tends to draw in people who resonate with it, and in my younger years, my aura was one of desperation, people-pleasing, and self-doubt. I didn't love myself, so it's no surprise that I attracted individuals who didn't love me either. We might not see it at the time – I certainly didn't – but others can sense it almost instantly.

In fact, many of my male friends have professed to being able to identify insecure women from a distance. It's almost impossible to describe in words, but there's a particular vibe we carry, a signal in some sense, that screams, *I'm unaware of the beauty I hold, someone please reassure me,* or *I don't value myself.* It took me so long to work this out. Even just a few years ago, after my mum passed away, I was in a relationship with a manipulative partner who kept me both distracted from my purpose and dependent on him and exterior sources of escapism.

It was a hard lesson in how love can be weaponized against you. But it's a lesson I'm grateful to have learned. I was able to walk away with the knowledge of why we should always recognize the strength that lies within us, especially during the challenging chapters of our lives.

In moments of vulnerability, when your life is clouded by sadness and desperation, it's all too easy for the wrong people to appear as saviors, like knights in shining armor.

These are individuals who wouldn't usually have proximity to you, but in a weakened state, you might inadvertently grant them access. And before you know it, you can become spellbound and reliant on them, instead of drawing from your own well of strength.

Unfortunately, these toxic relationships are so, so common. I see them everywhere around me – not just among the people I know, but even among complete strangers. Spend a few minutes on Reddit, run a Google search, or tune into a relationship podcast and it's evident that so many people sacrifice or lose large chunks of their lives to harmful relationships.

We've all heard those stories of people who've spent years, if not decades, with someone they're not equally yoked with, only to have an epiphany at a later stage, when they finally realize, *Oh my god, I've been a host to this parasite for most of my life.* And yes, I know 'parasite' is such a terrible word to use to refer to somebody, but when a relationship depletes your energy, sucks the best years out of you, and leaves you standing in front of the mirror looking visibly drained, what else can we call it? It's shocking and deeply upsetting, knowing you've lost so much time to somebody who wasn't worth it. And of course, once you recognize this loss with clarity, it's only natural to want to grieve.

Why it's so easy to punish ourselves

It's natural and incredibly easy to fall into the trap of self-punishment once we gain some distance and clarity from our mistakes. I found it hard not to do this after leaving that unhealthy relationship in my 20s.

I couldn't comprehend how oblivious I had been and constantly berated myself for what felt like a prolonged act of self-harm.

It was difficult not to completely grieve for my past self, even as I was trying to cultivate self-love. However, we need to keep in mind that settling for relationships that fall short is a common mistake that so many of us make. One that's human, relatable, and universal. It's not a unique experience that transforms us into 'failures.' Going through these experiences will teach us something valuable, provided we are willing to acknowledge and act on those lessons.

Taking valuable life lessons from our negative experiences

If we do the work and commit to building a strong and respectful relationship with ourselves, we can accomplish two crucial things. First, we can break free from relationships that drain us. Second, and perhaps more importantly, we can avoid repeating the same mistakes. There's that famous saying, sometimes attributed to Einstein: 'Insanity is doing the same thing over and over again and expecting different results.' This can easily be applied to the repetitive patterns we often find ourselves stuck in when it comes to unhealthy relationships.

Healthy relationships don't demand you shrink or dim your light for the other person to feel validated, superior, or comfortable. Healthy relationships don't require you to ignore your own needs, or to bury your desires or passions. Healthy relationships don't leave you feeling inadequate.

Bending over backward eventually causes our backs to break. I've come to understand that a healthy relationship relies on open communication, honesty, and a balanced exchange of love and care. We have a duty to take care of and protect ourselves. So, if we've finally woken up to the red flags we've been ignoring and realized that we've invested in the wrong person, then that's a moment for applause, not one for self-criticism. We've *already paid* a heavy price for settling for a love that isn't good enough, with the time that has already been spent.

If we've left a damaging relationship, we mustn't deplete ourselves even further by mentally and emotionally chastising ourselves after the fact. After all, we can't rewrite history, but we can influence our future. And we should celebrate the fact that we've reached a level of self-awareness that prepares us to be truly seen and loved by someone else, even if that moment hasn't arrived yet. Because when genuine love does find us, it is the purest gift we can ever receive.

Think

It's OK, and completely valid, to mourn the time you lost in an unhealthy relationship. However, it's not productive to let that grief become a self-destructive force that drags you down even further.

Ask

Put yourself in the shoes of a close supportive friend. If someone close to you just ended a bad relationship, what would you say to them? Would you chastise them for their choices? Or would you provide grace, understanding, and compassion, and encourage them to forgive themselves?

Do

Write down five qualities that you love and cherish in one of your closest friends. Don't think too hard about it, just the first ones that occur to you. Now read them back. If you're in a relationship, do these qualities mirror those of your partner? If you're single, do these attributes align with what you'd seek in a future partner?

Guess what? They should, on both counts.

We accept that it's OK to outgrow friendships

Reflecting on what I've written about so far in this book, it becomes clear how pivotal friendships have been in shaping my life.

I've talked about friends, the roles they've played, their influence, and the experiences I've gone through with them far more than I've mentioned romantic connections! And to be honest, I think that's a pretty universal experience for all of us. I'm not saying that our relationships with our significant others aren't important to our lives – of course they are – but sometimes, the inherent value and powerful impact of our friendships get overshadowed by the intensity and drama that often accompany love and romantic entanglements.

My friends have brought invaluable insights...

My friends have enriched my life in countless ways, including offering invaluable insights into diverse cultures and communities. Growing up in a predominantly white area, I never overthought the concept of diversity. I was young. I didn't give it a second thought. I had many friends, some were Welsh, some were Irish, and some were English. My mum instilled a strong sense of pride and awareness of my Trinidadian roots, so I knew who I was and where I came from. Plus, on Sundays, I would attend a West Indian Pentecostal church, which was full of Jamaicans.

But everything shifted when I entered secondary school and became friends with girls from various religious and cultural backgrounds. Through Nowsheen, I gained an understanding of the Muslim community, and Vanessa taught me about Filipino culture. Jamiila gave me my first insight on an interracial upbringing, as her mother was Finnish and her father was Jamaican. Emma was British-born and bred, with a liberal outlook. She was the first person I ever knew who openly swore around her mum – something I couldn't even envision myself doing without swift repercussions! I admired the freedoms she had.

My circle expanded even more during my time at college, where I made my first Caribbean and African friends. I learned a lot more about Blackness through these friends – our music, our language, our collective experiences. These friends, hailing from different parts of London, introduced me to new slang, hairstyles, and perspectives that were different from those in my local area. This opened my eyes even further.

The most influential friend I've had, though, is an elder I met through my mum's church. She's now 89 years old and my personal source of wisdom and spirituality. Like my mum's parents, she was part of the Windrush generation. She even served as a maternal figure to my mum, and supported Mum throughout her early 20s, as she found refuge in the church to escape the horrors of her abusive home. She approached me when I was young, offering a listening ear during a disruptive Sunday School lesson (Sunday School bored the shit out of me), and has been my best friend ever since.

Mum confided in her about the gifts I'd been blessed with as a child and about the things I would envision, proclaim, or dream. Through Millie Scarlet, I've gained not only invaluable insights around Christianity but also a newfound confidence in my spiritual gifts that she never downplayed or ridiculed me for having. She showed me that friendships aren't just something you share with people of your own age, but are deep spiritual connections that can be forged between any two people.

...but also, deep heartbreak

However, I've made so many mistakes with friendships, too. So, so many. I've discussed many of them throughout this book. Whether it was prioritizing others over myself, allowing people to exploit my early successes, aligning myself with those who didn't share the same values as me, or tolerating being treated like a meal ticket, I had my blind spots. I didn't realize how fortunate I was to have authentic, caring individuals around me until I found myself around those who were the opposite.

I still stumble. I still make mistakes and misjudgments. I've allowed low-vibrational people to be close to me and those I loved, simply because I trusted too early. This decision resulted in my mother being exposed to high levels of stress and threatening behavior during her last months, simply because I failed to vet someone who I classed as a friend.

I see now that my lingering need to be liked attracted the wrong people to me. But that doesn't mean the emotional toll is any less when you realize they're not your true friends. I'm beginning to recognize that the pain I carry won't disappear until I decide to make the changes needed for growth – and this extends to friendships as well. Unlike romantic relationships, the feeling when friendships end is different. You don't 'break up' or 'move on' from friends, you spiritually outgrow them.

Understanding that some friendships aren't meant to last

There's a well-known saying, claiming that friends enter your life for a season, a reason, or a lifetime. While I can't take credit for that wisdom, I find immense value in the message it conveys. After all, there isn't much guidance out there for how to accept and navigate a friendship that has naturally come to an end. We are all so focused on giving and receiving advice on how to deal with our love lives that we have no idea what to do when the state of our friendships is in turmoil.

My interpretation of this saying is that it's essential to understand not every friendship is meant to be a permanent fixture in our lives. Some will stand the test of time, which I find beautiful – there's something incredibly rich about sustaining a deep connection with someone who's known you through various phases of life. However, not everyone is destined to accompany you throughout your entire journey, and that's perfectly fine. I firmly believe that everyone we meet serves a purpose for a specific season in our lives, and every person comes with lessons that were intended for us to learn. And sometimes friendships naturally expire, not necessarily because either party did something 'wrong,' but simply because their season has come to an end.

Why friendships fade

There are countless reasons why friendships evolve or drift apart. It could be as simple as life's commitments getting in the way of establishing quality time together, or maybe you've come to realize that the common ground you once shared isn't as solid as it once seemed. However, it doesn't have to be any of these. It can just be a feeling inside that the connection you once cherished isn't there anymore.

The important thing is that you recognize and honor this realization, and don't prolong the process of growing apart from people. It's not healthy to cling onto a bond that's naturally coming to an end. Acceptance is key. At some point, we must understand that not everyone is meant to stay in our lives forever. Some people are in our lives for a season, and then the relationship gently fades as you both grow apart. It's natural.

The process of separating from a friend can be painful. It can bring a mix of different emotions, and there's no one right way to navigate this. What remains important, though, is the respect and care you show in the process. Don't just ignore their texts and calls. If it's clear that your paths are separating, then allow this to happen peacefully. Move forward and take with you the wisdom gained from the time spent together and send them off with kindness. It's up to you to decide how to do that, but afford that person the esteem you would hope to receive yourself. And you never know – if life decides that you both have more to learn from each other, you might reconnect again.

Recognizing when a friendship harms us

Of course, there are times when we inevitably encounter friendships that seem enriching on the surface but, upon closer examination, reveal themselves to be detrimental to our mental and emotional well-being. It's vital for us to be able to acknowledge these negative influences and have the courage to remove ourselves from these situations.

I've shared in this book about my experiences with people I once considered friends, who did more harm than good, and who enabled my worst habits for their own comforts. It's a hard truth knowing that sometimes those who we count on to lift us up may actually benefit from our decisions to limit ourselves and play small, thus perpetuating our unhealthy habits. That's why it's imperative to safeguard our inner peace and protect ourselves from those questionable friends who take pleasure in our downfalls rather than our accomplishments and happiness.

Life is far too short and precious to waste time justifying the actions of those who don't have our best interests at heart.

Everything I outlined in the previous chapter, about what love *isn't,* can be applied to friendships, too. Remember that a healthy and balanced friendship is a two-way street, something that promotes joy and elevates your spirit. It shouldn't ever leave you feeling diminished, low, less-than, or constantly subsuming your own needs.

When we have true friends in our lives, they can bring such light and support to us, especially during periods of vulnerability. After my mum's passing, it was the support and compassion from my friends, spanning from Trinidad to the UK, that carried me through. They provided not only emotional support but also offered financial assistance and unreserved kindness – something that will remain etched in my memory forever.

That's why it's imperative to seek out connections with people who complement our lives and who genuinely care about us; because while the bond continues to strengthen, their role in your life shifts, too. They evolve from being an acquaintance to a friend to becoming one of your pillars of support. We need to identify the qualities and intentions of those who are close to us, and pay attention to how they make us feel, because their influence has the power to impact us positively or negatively.

Think

We can choose between friends who challenge us to evolve and those who enable us and are comfortable with us standing in a place of discomfort. Remember, our friends are our chosen family, the key word being *chosen*. We're under no obligation to stick with them if the connection is nonexistent.

Ask

Reflect on your relationships. Is there a sense of relief when you think about certain people who are no longer in your orbit? Or is there someone in your life whose presence leaves you feeling depleted? Dig deep into those feelings and ask yourself why you feel like this. Compare them with how you feel when you're around the friends who nourish and uplift your spirit. Is there a difference? If so, what sets them apart?

Do

If there's someone in your circle who you're questioning, or suspect deep down is not a true friend, take a pause from interacting with them for a while. Each week, jot down your emotions about their absence. Do you miss their presence and what they bring to your life, or is the space they once occupied now more peaceful? Act on your observations. Remember, you hold the power to let go of relationships that dim your light. Allow yourself the space to learn, break, rebuild, heal, and flourish.

We advocate for ourselves and step into our power

As I approached my 30s, I fell in love with a friend I had known for years. The honeymoon period was a blissful, beautiful exchange of sharing our inner worlds beyond anything we learned in our friendship.

He nursed me back to health during a period of significant loss, and to reciprocate, I gave him access to a few opportunities and helped him see the value within himself. When we discovered a mutual liking, falling in love felt natural. In my mind, that was it: I'd found my person, and all that was required of me now was to continue creating a life for myself. Unfortunately, as time passed, cracks began to show.

When we moved in together, little things would cause massive flare-ups. He was always transparent about his childhood and upbringing, revealing that he often felt like he didn't have a voice, and was an outcast in his family due to the dynamic between him and his parents.

His mother was abusive and his father was docile. After their divorce, his father left the family home, leaving my ex to face the brunt of his mother's anger. She did a range of different things to break him: She would idealize him in public and criticize him in private; feel resentful of his romantic relationships; subject him to emasculation; silence him; give him unrealistic household chores and then physically assault him when he failed to reach her expectations; and gaslight him while victimizing herself.

He always claimed that his father abandoned him but would always end by saying how much respect, honor, and admiration he had for his father. That's one thing I've noticed with adults who were abused or neglected as children: They always leave a little 'what-if' room for their parents. No matter their age. There's always room available for reconciliation with the hopes that their parents will one day change.

How rising above meant sinking below

The phrase 'stoop to conquer' means a strategic choice to humble oneself temporarily to achieve a greater purpose or to navigate through a challenging circumstance. My ex would always refer to his choice to tolerate his mother as a way of 'stooping to conquer,' and at first, I understood his reasonings based on what I'd witnessed growing up. Sometimes, maintaining your peace reigns supreme instead of squabbling over things we could ignore.

Throughout his life, my ex would absorb all the negative interactions with his mother and learned to make himself more palatable, but it didn't work, nor did it improve the mistreatment. Sometimes, we would hold space for each other to vent – I would walk around the room moaning about family who hurt me in the past, and he would reenact the argument and respond truthfully about what he wished he could confront his mother about.

In these moments, he was bold and courageous, speaking up and out clearly, qualities he felt he couldn't access or possess in real-life scenarios. It was evident that this version of himself was the person he aspired to become – someone who stood up for themselves. Still, anytime he and his mother would argue, he would lose the ability to articulate himself and end up stooping.

His choice to not address confrontational moments worried me, and I'd often ask him, 'Why don't you tell your mum the truth about how she makes you feel?' I'd question the impact this must be having on his mental health, but he would play my concerns down, instead referring to the Bible and quoting scripture to support his stance. His take was that he was rising above and remaining peaceful – *stooping to conquer*. But he wasn't peaceful, not inside, and eventually, not at all.

His behavior changed rapidly. He grew more and more frustrated, irritable, and angry. He was lashing out at friends and family. In his mind, everyone was against him, everyone else was to blame, and nobody respected him. He was in conflict with many people, none of whom were aware of it. He displaced the anger he held for his mother onto everyone that surrounded him.

The challenge in trying to find our voice

How often have you been in a similar situation? You find yourself in a moment where every fiber of your being is telling you to speak up for yourself, to claim your space, and make your voice heard. Yet, despite your internal cries, you're overtaken, succumb to self-doubt, and silence yourself instead?

This struggle isn't foreign to me, either. I can't tell you how often I've been there. There have been so many times when I chose to stay quiet instead of honoring my truth. Then, in the aftermath, I felt riddled with disappointment. I replayed the events in my mind, tormenting myself with endless versions of 'what ifs,' imagining all the things I could have said, or the actions I should have taken, if only I'd had the courage to see it through.

It's awful, isn't it? The frustrations that we have with ourselves, while those 'what-if' thoughts continue to invade our minds. We get stuck in a loop of self-berating. Promising ourselves that if it happens again, *this time we will speak up.* But when the issue resurfaces, and reality hits, in that moment, our courage fails us again.

Countless times I've found myself in the same loop of wanting to say something but silencing myself instead. Eventually, this self-sabotaging habit became so ingrained that it led to a recurring negative belief that my life is better lived on the sidelines.

I convinced myself that I was simply not someone who could speak up and that was the narrative I accepted. But it didn't make me feel settled, nor did it bring me any form of peace. Instead, I grew resentful within and directed it toward those I believed had silenced me. This feeling within would bubble up like lava and solidify inside me.

Why staying silent causes us inner turmoil

The truth is that suppressing our feelings can create internal conflicts far more harmful than the external disputes we're attempting to dodge. There's a saying that illustrates this vividly: 'Resentment is like drinking poison and expecting the other person to die.' It's a potent metaphor for the turmoil we inflict upon ourselves.

When we choose to silence our voice and bury these negative, uncomfortable feelings, they don't simply disappear – they begin to fester within.

Invariably, they find a way back to the surface, often through an inappropriate outburst. This is because harbored resentment builds up pressure within, and when it erupts, we have little control over its expression. This is exactly why it's important to speak your truth.

When we hold our emotions back, we're not just keeping quiet; we're actively undermining our own sense of balance and peace.

These emotions, when kept locked away, start to churn within us, producing anger, resentment, and deep-seated disappointment. This emotional turmoil can lead us to live in a constant state of unhappiness and anxiety. The danger is that this can then pave the way for chronic stress and even depression. This is not mere speculation; it's something I've personally witnessed, especially with the ex I mentioned earlier.

Even my own mother suffered deeply from this. By choosing not to address the toxic and harsh behaviors within her own family for years, Mum stored all that pain and turmoil inside herself, and accumulated a lot of internal stress, which detrimentally affected her peace of mind.

The misleading belief that avoidance is self-care

But what leads us to this point? Why do we shy away from confrontation, even when we've felt the ramifications of avoidance before? Well, there can be several reasons behind it.

For one, dodging confrontation can give us a false sense of safety. We cling to the belief that we're protecting ourselves from harm by not engaging in difficult exchanges that can feel immediately uncomfortable. But by resisting this momentary discomfort, we're setting ourselves up for a more pain in the long term.

Avoiding confrontation can also be deeply rooted in a perceived fear of rejection – a fear that many of us carry from past experiences where speaking our truth resulted in a negative response that left us feeling worse. It's also reinforced by societal norms, where politeness and preventing awkward situations are prioritized above honesty and transparency. Although these intentions may be honorable, they can lead people to avoid being truthful with each other, and delay honest conversations, resulting in additional misunderstandings and frustrations.

No matter the circumstances, dodging our problems is not an effective method for managing our difficult moments.

After all, I've said it before, but I'll say it again: Everything we run away from resides within, so regardless of how far we stray, the pain will always come with us.

Furthermore, when we hold our emotions back, we're not just keeping quiet; we're actively undermining our own sense of balance and peace. In doing so, we grant our anxieties more territory in our minds, allowing them to fester and expand into something that will be harder to remove.

From silence to strength: The power of speaking your truth

The good news is that transformation is always within our grasp. Healing begins the moment we choose to express ourselves with clarity and intention. I've changed, my mum changed, and my past love, who endured great challenges with his mother, eventually changed.

In the wake of his breakdown, he embraced therapy, reconnected with his friends, and began the process of evolving past that angrier version of himself. He grew tired of lashing out at the people who loved him, and his communication took on a newfound strength. He advocated for himself, became firmer in his expressions, started standing up for himself, and reached a point in his life where he no longer feared losing those who only contributed stress and confusion to his life. By utilizing his voice, he stepped into a space of liberation.

This was the healthiest version of him that I had ever witnessed. Watching his transformation allowed me to adopt a few lessons myself. I learned the importance of remaining firm in my truth and understanding that to be courageous means ensuring that my voice is heard. Over time, standing my ground became addictive.

There's a unique beauty in knowing you have the strength to stand alone and the courage to go against the crowd.

Those who had benefited from my previous compliance became very uncomfortable and silently removed themselves from my life. At the same time, the people who poured confidence into me over the years beamed with pride every time I spoke up for myself. It was empowering and, for the first time, I felt the weight of my words, and I realized they had the authority to reshape my life.

I'll be honest: This change isn't necessarily the easiest thing to do. It's an unsettling, heart-pounding feeling, the moment we decide to react differently and stand up for ourselves. But this process also has the potential to be the beginning of a significant character rebirth; because when we foster self-awareness, we begin to see the patterns in our behavior that contribute to our own suffering – patterns of self-sabotage that we have the power to change.

And by finding our voice and speaking up for ourselves, not only do we advance our own healing, but we also enlighten those around us, too. Because, in our silence, we never truly communicate the impact other people's words have over our lives. They may be completely oblivious to the stress they inflict. By articulating our feelings with clarity and consideration, we create the opportunity for mutual understanding and collective healing.

Think

We experience internal conflict and pain because we're being called to evolve and shift our approach to certain patterns in our life. Only we can make this change through bringing our internal conflicts out into the open.

Ask

What are you afraid will happen if you speak up? Will it really be any worse than the inner torment you already put yourself through? If you think, *yes, it will,* then ask yourself why. Or are you just projecting a worst-case scenario?

Do

Think about a recent situation where you felt resentful toward the other person but didn't vocalize it. Write down what you wish you'd said during the interaction.

Remember to keep it clear and focus on your emotional response, not what you imagine the other person thinks or feels. Say it out loud a few times, and edit it, tweak it, until it sounds completely natural to you.

Practice saying it out loud until it becomes second nature. This will help remove some of the defensive fear and unpreparedness for when you next see the person in question. Then say it! You can do it; I know you can.

Reflection

As we turn the page to the final part of our journey, I understand that the points we've just explored – where we've unearthed our own unhealthy patterns of self-sabotage and discussed how to navigate through them – may not have been easy to read. If you found it challenging to digest, or difficult to implement the changes in your life, that's OK. In fact, it's more than just 'OK' – it's commendable. And it's essential to recognize your efforts, too.

As I've mentioned throughout this book, the act of confronting our truths reveals to us how ugly, complex, and uncomfortable that process can be. But as the saying goes, 'Healing comes in waves,' and we have the ability to cultivate ease into our journey by transforming choppy waters into a serene, free-flowing river, helping us to arrive at a place of contentment and calm.

I hope reading this section has reinforced the concept that we are, in essence, the true architects of our personal journey toward healing. Yes, we can seek and receive support from professionals like therapists and life coaches, and we can gain strength from the care of family and our wider community – the people who genuinely wish us well. And perhaps you might even discover some measure of peace in the words I've put down on these pages. However, the core truth remains that the crucial work of healing is a task we must undertake ourselves.

The discomfort we encounter as we navigate the complexities of life is inevitable – it challenges us to confront our emotions and responses directly. It's through facing these challenges that we ripen our inner strength. This resilience, once developed, doesn't just help us cope with the current difficulties that arise; it empowers us for future adversities, nurturing a strength within that we might not have imagined possible.

Speaking from my own life's journey, I can affirm that with every new challenge I faced, the more adept I became at overcoming them. As we learn and grow from each obstacle, life feels increasingly within our control. This transformation is profound; it's about learning a new way of living, one that we consciously choose and then continue to choose every day, cultivating our resilience and well-being.

3 how we nurture and protect our hearts

In this final part, we bring together all the insights gained and steps taken, and integrate them into our daily lives. The goal is to move beyond making sporadic efforts that eventually fade away and instead, create permanent changes in our lives. Because The Good Quote has helped me shape my life, as well as millions of others', quotes form the bedrock of this section. They offer simple yet powerful truths, offering gentle reminders for our healing journey.

At the end of each chapter, there'll be a couple of short paragraphs for you. They're crafted to remind you how every insight we're going to cover is designed to both nurture and protect your heart. We'll learn about developing our intuition and kindness, living with intention, the art of setting boundaries, the importance of understanding the essence of time, the power of building genuine connections, the courage to embrace our destiny, and ultimately, the wisdom of letting go.

We listen to
our intuition

Growing up, I was a weird kid, and it was something I was always deeply aware of. It manifested in many different, mystical ways.

For example, I would regularly have prophetic lucid dreams. I always sensed unseen presences, and when I was around pregnant women, I always knew what sex their babies would be. What's more, I often had a premonition when someone was close to passing away. It sounds crazy, but it's my truth.

When I confided these experiences to my mum, I think they frightened her; she would worry about how others might perceive this aspect of my personality. Frankly, it caused me a little anxiety, too. However, despite her own fears, Mum always reassured me. 'It doesn't matter baby,' she'd say. 'As your mum, it's my responsibility to learn who you are and to ensure that I'm guiding you in the right direction.'

Being shown I could embrace who I am

It wasn't until I became friends with Millie (the community elder, a descendant of the Maroons in Jamaica, who I introduced earlier on page 139) that I learned how to embrace this side of myself. I found a confidante in Millie, and she became someone with whom I shared these intense and powerful experiences that often left me feeling overwhelmed. Millie's empathy and wisdom, gained from personal experiences, transformed my perspective. What was once a source of embarrassment became a trait I was proud to embrace. She taught me the significance of owning my gifts with confidence, teaching me not to dim my light, simply because it deviated from what others would consider 'normal.'

In addition, empathy has always been a defining part of who I am. Maybe a lot of it stems from my mum's teachings on how to be a compassionate person, which I learned to practice as I watched her navigate her family abuse. Or maybe it's simply a core part of my being – it's hard to say. What I know for sure is that this profound level of empathy is one of the main reasons I founded The Good Quote. My goal was to use social media as a platform to create a community where I offer emotional support through quotes and literature.

Connecting with others is something I naturally excel in. Some people bond and build connections in various ways like music, hobbies, or sports, but for me, when it comes to emotions, that's where I thrive. Sit me down with any stranger and within 20 minutes, I'll be able to tell you everything about what's on their mind. There's a certain level of trust that people have in me, and it's a responsibility I've always been reminded to hold with honor. I don't take it lightly at all.

Connecting and communicating with our intuition

I've come to understand that learning to embrace these qualities about myself was really about tuning in to my intuition. Intuition is a term we hear often, a concept introduced to us early in life, yet it defies a simple explanation. For me, intuition is simply the emotional bond we share with our innermost selves. I don't think it manifests the same in all of us. After all, we're all having different human experiences. At its core, intuition is an instinctive awareness of our own personal truths. A subconscious guide that directs us closer toward where we belong, while steering us clear of the potential dangers that lie in our paths.

Drawing from my own journey, I've grown to see my intuition as a compass for this physical world. I believe it's a growing strength that flourishes when we choose to develop a healthier relationship with it. It's about gently pushing our ego aside and allowing our intuition to exist freely, and by doing so, it becomes clear to see why this superpower should be honored, listened to, and handled delicately. Its profound ability of foresight is something we eventually learn to depend on, reminding us that its main purpose is to serve and guide.

However, when we turn a blind eye to the warnings from our intuition, we do ourselves a huge disservice. We betray our higher selves. But here's the thing, our intuition is patient. It waits, and in the midst of this, it teaches us a valuable lesson: the importance of trusting that inner voice, especially as we face the aftermath of ignoring it. When we choose to remain loyal to this powerful inner voice, it helps us distinguish it from the voices of other negative influences. Many feel they need solid reasons to trust their intuition, but the beauty lies in simply trusting it first; the logic of *why* reveals itself later. This, I've learned, is how our intuition tests our faith – revealing its wisdom once we're truly committed to listening.

How does your intuition communicate with you? Are you the type who reflects in silence, only to have your visions or train of thoughts suddenly interrupted by cut-throat hypothetical scenarios – the what-might-happen consequences if you were to ignore your feelings? Or maybe your intuition is more like a loud, internal cry, causing your heart to jump and skip a beat as an electric shock bolts through your system, and adrenaline forces you to stop in your tracks? Or maybe it's a series of reminders, through gentle whispers that slowly fade away as time passes? Or are you someone who experiences physical manifestations of your intuition, where it feels like fingers intertwine through your gut and then clench into a fist to get your attention anytime your mind subconsciously drifts away from what you're occupying yourself with at the time?

No matter which of these expressions resonates with you the most, or if your personal experience is completely different, the truth is we all have these moments. Have you ever contemplated why these things happen? Why we suddenly become so attuned to these unfamiliar, uncomfortable vibrations? It's simply your intuition doing its best to safeguard you.

When we acknowledge these feelings for what they truly are – a sacred signal from within, informing us that there's an imbalance that needs addressing – it becomes easier to recognize the soul's call for healing.

Really, all we need to do is *listen*.

Dealing with difficulties – and doubt

I understand that sometimes telling people this can feel a bit like *easier said than done*. There's a certain mystique around intuition; the concept itself is clouded in so much vagueness, coupled with a heavy weight of expectation, which can cause people to feel anxious about tapping into it. We're often led to believe that our intuition should manifest in a certain way, like a sudden revelation or a moment of profound clarity, where we stop in our tracks and go, *Of course!* And when our experience doesn't align with this, we might believe that we've failed, as if we're lacking in intuition overall. But the truth is, intuition is part of us all. Everybody has it. We just need to take the pressure off and take away the noise that surrounds it.

We're often surrounded by well-wishers, showering us with their expectations or unsolicited advice, which can cloud our judgment and leave us more confused than ever. When we have a decision to make and aren't sure of which direction to go in, this constant barrage of opinions can cause us to doubt ourselves. We struggle to connect with our instincts and become frustrated at ourselves for not having immediate clarity on what steps to take next.

Navigating through this involves reshaping how we react to these emotions. Doubt, at its core, is just another form of our intuition, under a different guise, trying to communicate with us. By softly welcoming in the energy of doubt, allowing it a temporary space in our lives to express its deepest concerns, we can develop a better understanding and create an alternative approach to the problems it believes we will face ahead.

When doubt arrives on our path, our initial response is often engulfed in fear, anxiety, and mental exhaustion, as we think, *Oh no, why am I so unsure about this?* But instead of suppressing these feelings – which ironically tends to amplify them in our minds – we can choose a different approach. By shifting our relationship with doubt from opposition to collaboration, we open up a more constructive and beneficial way moving forward.

Honoring doubt to find our true feelings

We shouldn't turn away from doubt. I don't believe it's an enemy, as every emotion has its place and a function that was intentionally designed to help support us as we navigate our way through this human experience. We can listen to what our doubt is telling us. It acts as a checkpoint on our path to connecting with our intuition and building confidence in our own abilities. At times, doubt may attempt to stop us moving forward, a manifestation of our fears, but at other times, it's a protective measure against potential harm. Regardless of its motive, it's always valuable to pay attention to what it has to say.

On my journey to overcoming self-doubt, increasing emotional awareness forced me to accept that when we're approaching the cusp of a personal breakthrough, life's distractions and doubt will intensify. It's frustrating, but it's a reality. In life, there will always be setbacks, which is why it's crucial to be emotionally vigilant and prepared. And being in tune with our feelings and reactions is just as important.

So, if you're finding it difficult to tune in or listen to your intuition, don't let it stress you out. And if you find yourself grappling with doubt, again, it's OK. Honor these emotions, as they've arrived for a reason. Jot down everything you're feeling, so you can clear your mind, and if possible, talk them through with a sympathetic ear (while not asking

When we turn a blind eye to the warnings from our intuition, we do ourselves a huge disservice. We betray our higher selves.

for solutions!). Examine these feelings candidly and ask yourself: *Why is this doubt here? Why has it shown up for me now?*

This is how we start the process of reclaiming our power, finding our footing, and reconnecting with our inner voice. It's about rebuilding the trust we have in ourselves. By working with our doubt rather than working against it, we can bring all these voices in alignment with our own capabilities and best intentions. After all, we're on the same team.

How intuition nurtures

When we listen to our intuition, we increase our self-belief, which is a significant part of how we survive and flourish. When we possess the conviction to approach anything that lands on our paths without losing ourselves through the influence of others or the plague of our own thoughts, our hearts are strong.

How intuition protects

Those feelings of dread, panic, or doubt are only our intuition attempting to connect with us via any means possible. It's still an intuitive pull to listen to our instinct and follow our calling. We just have to work through these layers first.

We are kind to the unkindest parts of ourselves

I admit, I haven't always been the nicest person. As I've shared before, I was a bully in primary school – a part of my past I genuinely regret. But I've come to understand the roots of that behavior, which makes it easier to recognize in others – I was simply an angry and wounded child.

Not only did I not understand why my father was absent, but despite my mum's best efforts to safeguard me, I was exposed to her family's chaotic and harmful dynamic. You're already aware of the cruel words my grandfather said to me. But it wasn't just him. Other family members inflicted pain, too. My aunt frequently tried to dim my light by reminding me that my personality was too much, my presence was exhausting for those around me, my dreams were unattainable, and that I contributed nothing of value to conversations.

These brutal words spoken over me would leave a long-lasting mark on my mind, slowly seeping into my subconscious. My inner dialogue turned negative, mirroring the treatment I received, and I became accustomed to speaking to myself like an enemy, because growing up, that's what was fed to me by these family members. My relationship with Mum was beautiful – she truly was my best friend – but these other words spoken eroded my self-esteem and contributed to an internal dialogue that repeatedly told me that I was worthless, ugly, unloved, and strongly disliked for no other reason than existing.

The destructive power of a negative inner voice

Now, I recognize that my childhood behavior labeled as 'naughty' was actually a reflection of the voices that made me feel inadequate. Yet, as an adult, this harsh internal dialogue only became more deeply pronounced.

Living with this relentless cycle of self-critique was like hosting a negative inner voice that celebrated my downfalls and perpetuated my fears and insecurities. This inner voice had been festering within me for years, silently taking note of everything said against me and saving it as ammunition for future opportunities to attack. It's one of the biggest contributors to how I broke my own heart by reinforcing negative perceptions of myself and my own abilities.

Rebuilding my life and learning to live beyond fear and self-sabotage meant I had to confront this persistent negative inner voice face first. I knew that to work on myself meant I would need to tackle one of the hardest obstacles that I face daily: my mind.

Because honestly, living with this voice was *exhausting*. I yearned to reside in a mind that would speak to me compassionately. I wanted to enjoy having beneficial conversations with my inner self, embracing life's curiosities and unknowns. I wanted to try something new and feel encouraged instead of belittled. I wanted to experience the freedom of living in harmony with myself. I wanted to respond to a loving voice, not a critical one.

So, I deeply resonate – on a spiritual level – with the struggle of what it feels like to be a host to a negative inner voice. If you're experiencing this, know that you're not alone, I promise. This voice might be silent to others, but to us, it screams loudly, and escaping it seems impossible. How do you escape something that resides in your own head?

Sometimes, I'm shocked by the cruelty of my inner voice's words. I often wonder, *Who does this voice belong to? Why has it found refuge in my mind?* I believe this is a shared experience for many, even if it's something we rarely discuss with others.

We shouldn't underestimate or overlook the profound effect that this silent, yet piercing internal dialogue has on our lives. To be the host of an unfriendly inner voice is to live each day with internal storms that take comfort in lowering our self-confidence and overall peace of mind.

When we allow ourselves to be guided by a voice that intentionally echoes our doubts and fears, unconsciously, we create a pattern of undermining ourselves and our daily efforts.

Our inner dialogue shapes the way we perceive ourselves, impacts our emotional well-being, and influences how we navigate challenges. It can either help or hinder our relationships with others, our decision-making processes, our ability to grow, the ways we strive toward betterment, and our overall satisfaction.

So, if you're living with an unkind, belittling, and disparaging internal voice, I know how bad it can be! The question is, how do we quieten it and begin treating ourselves with more kindness? The first step is to understand the origins of this negativity because, after all, awareness is the beginning of invoking change.

Why our negative voice doesn't speak the truth

It's important to remember that this voice is not a true reflection of who we are, nor does it belong to us. This voice isn't all-powerful, all-seeing, all-knowing. It's simply a pest that has become comfortable in a space that we took too long to evict it from. I believe it's essential to remind ourselves of this often, because one of the traps of a negative internal voice is playing into the assumption that it's correct.

For some reason, we afford it a godlike level of intelligence. We listen to it and take in everything it says to us as unassailable truth. Yet we wouldn't do that to any other voice, would we? We know others are fallible and capable of making mistakes and misjudgments, and we acknowledge the same about ourselves, too. So, why do we presume that this internal voice is always 100 percent correct in its criticisms and negativity?

Our inner voices are often just reflections of our deepest wounds and internalized trauma: that's it. In the same way that my inner voice mirrored the toxicity of my family, your negative internal dialogue likely echoes your own hurts or ongoing wounds. Understanding that is the first step to removing some of its power and shifting the role it plays in our lives, because our inner voice can also be a powerful tool for positive reinforcement.

I reflect on times when my relationship with my inner voice was healthy, in both the past and the present. I fondly remember the overwhelming sense of warmth I felt anytime I developed the courage to accomplish something new, and my inner voice supported me with compliments and positive affirmations, keeping me motivated. There's so much liberation in that feeling.

Learning to speak to ourselves with compassion, not criticism

Rewiring our brains to silence the critical, unkind voice is a battle in itself. But once we discover the origins of these negative thoughts, we have a responsibility to heal and dissolve them. We break our hearts every time we succumb to the taunts, but welcoming in a constructive, kinder inner dialogue can transform our human experience. Through its validation, we can cultivate enough resilience to pursue our deepest ambitions and embrace anything that lands on our path.

There are no simple, universal solutions to emptying the mind of negative thoughts. If there were, it would be common knowledge. *Everyone* would be using them, and our emotional struggles would be a thing of the past. However, there are strategies we can employ to stop toxic thoughts from holding us to ransom.

First, we need to acknowledge and accept their existence and then delve into their origins. Once we've understood that negative thoughts are merely a symptom of a belief system that requires challenging, we can then start to speak to ourselves more kindly.

It might feel strange at first, especially if we're not accustomed to using softer words to address ourselves. Yet it's vital to be mindful of our internal monologue, just as we would be in our language when speaking to a loved one. We wouldn't use spiteful words against them, so why do it to ourselves? Let's replace these harsh criticisms with supportive suggestions, select better words to describe ourselves, and be ready to challenge our inner voice whenever it goes against us.

Remember, the negative voice is not omnipotent. It's just a manifestation of our trauma seeking attention and trying to be heard. Let's commit to responding to this voice with kindness, and start changing the way in which we speak to ourselves.

How a kind inner voice nurtures

True liberation starts and ends in our mind. We imprison ourselves when we allow the voice of trauma to overpower us. By denying the attention it craves, we start to heal our wounds. We can transform these mirrors into windows, allowing the power of our inner light to radiate, creating a healthier narrative.

How a kind inner voice protects

When that inner voice speaks, no one listens more attentively to it than we do. So, when we work on strengthening our internal dialogue to be supportive and understanding, we work on strengthening our hearts, too.

We live with intention

It's amazing when profound moments strike us. For me, one of my most transformative realizations occurred while I was in an Uber, stuck in traffic in central London. It might not seem like the ideal setting for an epiphany, but bear with me.

Here's the scene: I was in a dark place at the time. I was using the guise of being busy to avoid confronting my own issues. I was building The Good Quote, obsessively spending hours each day online. As I've mentioned before, this made me feel robotic and disconnected from the real world, as well as overwhelmed by my own unhappiness. I felt as if I had no control over my life and was just drifting through the days, which seemed pointless and empty.

All the love I'd felt for life was slipping through my fingers. I'd accumulated a large amount of pain and distress over the years, so the concept of 'unpacking' all of this and facing myself seemed too big a burden to bear. But I decided to start therapy regardless, and it was during this one session that I had an insight I'll never forget.

A moment when the world's beauty struck me

In that therapy session, I found myself shedding tears for the most part. As I spoke about my feelings of inadequacy and hopelessness, I realized I was engaging in a behavior that's become so common nowadays: keeping ourselves incessantly busy to avoid the pain. My habits were designed to distract me from my thoughts, and my vices effectively swallowed up any free time I had, so I never had the privilege of facing myself.

My therapist asked me when I'd last taken the time to truly absorb my surroundings, not glued to a screen, but just peacefully taking in the world around me, without distractions. Not constantly checking messages, or aimlessly scrolling. I was stunned to realize that I couldn't recall the last time I had simply looked up and marveled at the sky.

Then, a memory resurfaced: the moment in the Uber, stuck in traffic near Euston Station. What makes this story even more compelling is that I was being incredibly lazy and wasting a lot of money jumping into that car, rather than walking the distance. But I was sad, and my intuition prompted me to take that journey, so I obeyed. As we merged onto the main road, I'd suddenly felt the warmth of the sun spreading across my face. The entire sky was a multitude of deep, rich hues, and I became captivated by the colors that hovered above me. It was so beautiful, even the driver shouted out, 'Woah, now isn't that something to be thankful for?' I found myself agreeing with him, while being completely mesmerized by the view above.

As I reflected on this moment during therapy, I remembered how, as a child, I would chase sunsets with my mum during our evening summer walks after school. She would always be in a childlike awe, playfully accusing God of showing off, while giving thanks for such a beautiful display. It made me question how, in my adulthood, I'd become so engulfed in busyness that I forgot to participate in the simple pleasures that made life exciting.

Losing my time to distraction

I shared this memory with my therapist, Michael, and he gave me one simple but profound instruction. 'Right Meg – this week your homework is to practice the art of aligning your attention with your intentions,' he said. I paused, as it was the first time I'd heard that term – *aligning your attention with your intentions*. Then I sighed. This seemed impossible for me. After all, *how was I expected to do that when I was so busy?* My therapist asked me to break down my morning routine for him, so we could work through a plan.

Then the truth hit me: I didn't really *have* a morning routine. Each day began with an urgent search for my phone, to catch up on the overnight messages. Afterward, I would mindlessly scroll through social media apps, contaminating my thoughts with the opinions of other people before I even gave myself the chance to dwell on my own. I would actively play Russian roulette with my triggers, as I automatically flicked through content, not knowing what would be coming next. I could be watching a wholesome, funny video and in the next swipe, see glimpses of a school shooting. Time would start to slip away, and I was already disconnected from myself, immersed in various online worlds.

This realization was a huge wake-up call. How did I create the habit of making myself so easily accessible to others, without prioritizing time with myself first? Why was I exposing myself to that level of content first thing in the morning, when it surely wasn't healthy in the long run? And if our morning routine sets the intentions for the rest of the day, then how was this practice serving me? It wasn't.

Connecting with the privilege of living

We often overlook the blessing of waking up to a new day, a gift that, unfortunately, not everyone receives. You can wake up in the morning with no guarantee of seeing the end of the day and you can fall asleep at night with no guarantee of waking up in the morning. Yet, in our digitally saturated lives, many of us rob this moment of its beauty.

If you wake up with intention, you'll discover how euphoric it can be. For artists, it's a time of heightened creativity, simply because our thoughts are at their purest. And while the body adjusts to the transition from the dream state back into this reality, there's a precious opportunity to bridge our subconscious to the conscious mind, and download as many gifts as possible, before that energy fades away.

If you've ever had a dream that feels so vivid, but disappears as soon as you're fully awake, you'll know what I mean!

Through this process of therapy and remembering that special memory in the taxi, I understood that there was something important I could do in the morning which would positively impact the rest of my day: plan ahead. So, I created a routine, something simple that I could stick to. Social media had transformed my attention span into that of a goldfish, so I needed to keep this routine straightforward and brief, yet nourishing, too.

I made small, but important changes to my habits. Every night, as I wound down, I would allocate time to write down my intentions for the following day. I prepared my outfit in advance and lastly, I ensured that my phone was put on silent and left in another room, to avoid the temptation of mindless scrolling. Each morning, I'd wake up and acknowledge the new day by giving thanks through prayer. Then, I'd grab my journal (which I'd left on my bedside table, so it was easy to find!), and pour out my thoughts. It didn't matter if they made sense or not, I just wrote down whatever came to mind. I'd conclude my morning ritual with a little stretch and a 20-minute guided meditation – and yes, OK, I'd get my phone to do this part – which in the early stages of this practice simply gave me an extra 20 minutes of sleep!

Though there were initial challenges, and the temptation to return to aimless scrolling was strong, this routine gently restored my sense of control and reignited my overall excitement for life. The more I expressed gratitude for each morning that I was gifted and spent those quiet moments with myself, the more I gravitated toward the belief that my life served a purpose again.

Bringing intentional habits into your own life

Look, if you're skeptical about this, believe me, I understand. I used to react the same way whenever someone talked about 'living in the present moment.' For me, this was always a distant priority; I didn't want to interrupt my levels of so-called productivity. It felt like a chore and a privilege for those who had too much time on their hands. But that was because I was ill-informed. I didn't realize that a part of living intentionally was simply ensuring that you are present in *every* encounter.

I also understand that not everyone can reshape their mornings as I did. If you have children, early work hours, or other commitments from the moment you wake up, this routine might not be feasible for you. However, you can modify it. Instead of scrolling through Instagram while waiting for the kettle to boil, look out of the window and notice the world around you instead. You can move your phone out of the bedroom so that it's not the first thing you reach for when you wake up. You can stop whatever you're doing on your laptop for a moment, step away from your desk, and breathe, giving silent (or vocal) thanks for the good things you have in your life.

It's essential for our mental health to carve out time each day to pause and be present, to ground ourselves in the here and now.

Our daily commitments and the distractions we subscribe to often consume us so much that we risk losing sight of the other significant aspects of our lives. In a world filled with endless distractions, we have the chance to reclaim the beauty of connection and community.

How living with intention nurtures

We only get one shot at this life, in this body, as this person, with our story, surrounded by this collective, during this time. Where we are right now is the most important place we can be. Remembering this can help align us with the incredible world we live in.

How living with intention protects

We tend to live as if we're immortal, with the belief that tomorrow is guaranteed. That's human nature, but how can this illusion positively serve us and shape the relationship we have with today? By bringing ourselves into a more connected state, and being aware of how we spend our time, we start to protect our hearts from the mindless habits that hurt them.

We reclaim our time

In the previous chapter, I delved into the concept of time, and our tendency to treat tomorrow as a certainty, which it's not.

Every day, someone's time runs out and what's left behind are the people whose lives they touched, and their personal stories of victories, loves, and losses. When we lose someone, it's natural to mourn and reflect on how they invested their time, energy, and focus: *They were so kind; they always looked after so-and-so; they loved doing x; or she found such happiness going to this place or that.*

I realize this might sound a bit bleak – and I'm not suggesting that the idea of dying is an easy one to confront *at all*. It's mind-blowing for all of us. But for those who have lost someone significant, you'll know what I mean when I say it can be a real wake-up call. As we come to terms with their physical departure from this world, many of us are silently shaken by the reality of time slipping away and deep introspection starts to kick in.

We start to evaluate our own lives, assessing where we might be dedicating too much or too little time. We question whether we've been living with intention, truly enhancing our human experience, or not. There's a well-known saying nowadays: 'Nobody lies on their deathbed wishing they'd spent more time in the office.' It's become a bit of a cliché now, but the essence of that idiom is true. Time is precious.

How I reassessed the value of time

Learning the true value of time wasn't easy for me. As I've shared, I spent much of my life as a people pleaser. I would rearrange my schedule for others, invest all my energy into helping them, and do whatever it took to see them happy or successful, often neglecting my own boundaries. I mistook my selflessness with being 'good' and 'kind.' But no one reciprocated my level of exertion, and eventually it got too much for me.

A conversation with my mum helped me move forward in altering my behavior. She told me, 'Meggan, if you ever feel fatigued in the pursuit of helping others, then your efforts need revising. The correct way to show up for others is to be realistic with your capacity to give, and ensure that your kindness never comes at a detriment to yourself.'

Her words were wise, but it took me a while to unlearn these lifelong habits. I understand now that helping others should come from a place that aligns with our values, instead of being a means to receive validation from others – which is what I was needlessly searching for. Our ego should never take precedence over our heart, and in cases where it does, we're often left managing feelings of unappreciation, burnout, and resentment (that was me, too).

The significance of valuing the essence of time hit home even harder after my mum passed away. As I've mentioned, she finally prioritized herself and learned to live fully in her last six years. But after she transitioned, I wished beyond measure that she had come to that conclusion earlier and had more time to herself. She deserved it.

These hard lessons caused me to reevaluate how I perceived and used my time. I began setting boundaries on how I would extend myself to others and on how I spent my time with purpose. This became an act of self-love, and through it, I began to reclaim my time, little by little. But you don't need to experience a personal grief to enact this change, you just need to appreciate the preciousness of time. It's not limitless; it's invaluable and irreplaceable. When we value our time more, an innate sense of awareness kicks in that causes us to operate with more thought and intention. We're reminded that the time we have is sacred and finite.

The key to setting boundaries

There's no one-size-fits-all approach to setting boundaries. Our lives are unique, and what works for one person might not suit another. I've shared what worked for me. So much of it centered around not responding immediately to the demands of my phone. Not letting myself get instantly distracted and refocused by messages and alerts that interrupted – or rather, that I *let* interrupt – my life. This had all led to a distracted, surface-level existence in which I didn't believe I was worthy of attention and love, because my life was designed around servicing the needs of others. This had to change.

Learning to say 'no' was crucial. It's probably the most effective strategy in boundary-setting. Agreeing to things we don't want to do leads to resentment and exhaustion. We've all been there, saying 'yes' to something and immediately regretting it, feeling trapped by

Pretending we don't have needs doesn't make us easier to love.

our commitment, wondering *why on earth did I say OK? I don't want to/can't do that!*

However, reversing this pattern is possible, and it's a learned habit that becomes easier over time. If we pause before responding, resisting the urge to please people immediately, saying 'no' becomes less hard to do. And once you get into the routine of saying 'no' to things that don't serve your best interests, you naturally start applying the same level of standards to your relationships, and the practice of asserting your boundaries becomes simpler.

What's more, through this, we start to see ourselves as worthy of being protected; that our time is valuable because *we ourselves* are valuable.

The act of reclaiming our time resets the power dynamics in our relationships, which enables us to have more control over the direction of our lives. This, in turn, makes us more accountable to ourselves. Accountability is really all about personal responsibility. We take an inventory of our behaviors, and we can tap into the unconscious parts of our personality that led us to behave like this. When we're accountable, we can truly confront ourselves and the emotions we've been suppressing.

When I started to ask myself difficult questions – which I did through audio journaling, chatting into my phone – the feelings that came out left me utterly blindsided. It helped me understand the reasons behind my boundary-less behavior, and its impact on me. We can all be honest with ourselves through introducing boundaries, and making how we spend our precious time *our responsibility.*

Why boundaries aren't unkind

One thing I also want to address is the relationship between boundaries and kindness. It's so easy to perceive being accommodating as a form of love – after all, we're doing exactly what the other person wants. So, when we remove that accommodation, and put boundaries in place, it can feel as if we're being cruel. This is made worse if the people that benefited from our boundary-less existence don't respond well and try to make us feel guilty for changing.

Navigating this can be tough, and I sympathize dearly, having experienced it myself. There are real dangers to being too accommodating. It can project a sense of naivety, attracting those with harmful intentions, and leaving us susceptible to being taken advantage of. But pretending we don't have needs doesn't make us easier to love. And remember, reclaiming our time will only frustrate those who felt entitled to having full access to it.

We need to protect ourselves from those who create rough seas in our hearts.

Applying a boundary is not an act of unkindness. I've said this before, but it bears repeating: Our boundaries are designed to protect us from unsafe habits and environments, they are not an attack on the other person. Unconditional love is not synonymous with unconditional tolerance. Asserting your boundaries doesn't diminish the love you have in your heart for someone; you can love them to the moon and back – but in a healthier manner.

How boundaries nurture

Taking care of ourselves is not just a choice; it's a responsibility. This is why it's imperative to be wise with how we use our time and energy. Boundaries aren't about exclusion or cutting things out; they're about ensuring our actions and focus reflect our true intentions, allowing us to utilize our time in the most beneficial way possible.

How boundaries protect

Boundaries are there to safeguard us from harmful behaviors, whether they stem from within us or from others. When someone fails to respect your boundaries, it's important to reassess their role in your life and be prepared to step back if necessary. Remember, genuine people recognize and respect each other's boundaries – and the same applies to us respecting others' boundaries as well.

We trust the process, understanding that things take time

If you're reading this book in chronological order, and you've just finished the previous chapter, you may be looking at *this* chapter title and thinking, *What? Hang on a minute, Meggan. Didn't you just write about how precious time is, how we shouldn't waste it, and now you're discussing the importance of taking time?*

I don't blame you if that's your initial impression. It might seem contradictory at first, but hey, being contradictory is a part of being human. This chapter isn't about backtracking; it's about rethinking our approach to patience and the time it takes for things to unfold. It's about bringing our awareness toward the external pressures we place on ourselves to achieve certain goals by specific deadlines, the problems that arise from rushing, and how we can set ourselves back by being overly fixated on the destination, forgetting to appreciate and enjoy the journey.

I've been through a lot of low places in my life, as you know well by this point. In writing this book and reflecting on the root causes of this pain, I understand that some of it – in fact, a lot of it – came from a deeply ingrained belief that I hadn't fulfilled certain expectations within a certain time frame. And that by not doing so, I had failed, which spiraled into a deep lack of self-worth, leading to further issues. It's all interconnected.

So many of the obstacles I went through – dropping out of uni, lacking a focus for my career, depression, poor lifestyle choices – were all amplified by the pressure I put on myself. Not only was I living according to other people's expectations, but I was also gauging my success against their timelines – or what I perceived they'd achieved. I drove myself crazy comparing myself to others around me, and what they were doing at 21, 22, 24, 27... *whatever* age it was. And if I wasn't doing just as 'well' as they were, then that was it. I had nothing to show for my life, because I hadn't hit those key milestones 'on time.'

How society creates a pressurized time frame

This sense of urgency, especially when we're younger, consumes so many of us. I'm only 35 now, but as I move into a part of my life where I have more wisdom and experience to draw upon, I can look back and see how harmful this mindset was. It's sad, but so many of us rush through our youth trying to hit certain milestones. And it's not until we're older that we realize that the milestones aren't what's important, the process, the *journey* is.

In today's world, the pressure to rush through life chasing specific ideals is stronger than ever. Social media bombards us with images of friends and strangers, all accomplishing certain photogenic goals: endless holidays, shopping hauls, perfect relationships, beautiful bodies, getting married, having babies, hitting career highs. This influences our thinking, casting a shadow over our own aspirations, especially when we haven't reached them yet. We set strict deadlines for our dreams and berate ourselves when we don't meet them. I've witnessed this in my own life, and in the lives of those around me. We allow ourselves to be dominated by a superficial societal narrative that glorifies rapid accomplishments. This leads to a life driven by ego (remember this, from Part 1?), where external measures of success dictate our self-worth.

We can live with purpose at every age

One of the major problems with the relentless pursuit of being quick, being fast, being *first* is what happens after we achieve these goals. Because even if we *do* achieve these ambitions, then what next? Most so-called 'life goals' are packed into the first 40 years of our lives, so what happens after that?

We blast through our human existence packing in all these milestones that society has told us we should be reaching for, and then – what?

I believe this is why so many people end up having mid-life crises. All their dreams and goals are in the past, and they feel a sense of despair at realizing how much more life there is left, without any clear direction or focus.

Life doesn't have to unfold this way. The elders in my life, like Millie, the 89-year-old Jamaican Maroon-Chinese lady from my community, have shown me that we can still live with purpose and enjoy aspirations at any age. Millie *still* says she has dreams yet to fulfill. Isn't that inspiring? Another elder of mine, Alan Roberts, bought a Harley-Davidson bike at 70, and often takes long escapes to the shore – just him, his leather jacket, his new fiancée, and a bunch of supplies. He even gave Mum a ride once, and it was lovely to watch her excitement as she rode on the back of a bike for the first time.

I haven't had children yet, but it doesn't mean I won't. I never wanted to be a young mum, and watching the experiences of my friends who've had kids at different points has shown me there is no one 'perfect' age to become a parent, either. These diverse experiences have shown me that there's no need to rush, or overthink and stagnate.

Life can still surprise us and offer achievable goals, regardless of our age.

The timelines we impose on ourselves are restrictive and can lead to feelings of inadequacy and failure. They are fictitious and shouldn't dictate the course of our lives. Life isn't a race to achieve and then suddenly stop. Being around all these inspiring elders, and even observing my mum's final years, has taught me that living a rich life means living with intention, cherishing every year we're blessed with. It's not about feeling like a failure for the rest of your life simply because you didn't finish your degree by the age of 21.

Adopting this perspective has eased the anxiety I feel inside. By nurturing my mind and body, and staying healthy, I've learned there's no need to rush. I can enjoy the ride. We all can. Time is indeed precious, as I've said before, but that doesn't mean we should blaze through it; we should take our time and start treasuring it.

How being patient nurtures

Life is meant to be lived and should flow freely into each new stage. Embracing patience in our progress is not something to fear. As long as we're committed to the work that needs to be done for us to evolve, and stay true to ourselves, we're on the right path.

How being patient protects

When we fast-track life, staying fixated only on goals, we lose sight of the essence of time. Remember, there's no medal for being first!

We recognize the power of forgiveness

In the introduction of this book, I discussed the immense strength in vulnerability. How opening ourselves up and embracing our vulnerable side is a superpower, not a sign of weakness.

In my experience, there's nothing more vulnerable than forgiving somebody for the pain and hurt they've caused you in the past. And this is what happened with my grandfather.

As you might remember, my mum and I had distanced ourselves from my grandfather due to his abusive behavior and the hurtful words he directed at me when I was a child. He truly was a horrible man who treated his family horrendously. So, his reemergence into our lives was initially met with strong resistance from me.

The reunion happened unexpectedly. My mum had started to adopt an easier way of life by reducing her hours at work following her first battle with cancer. She led a simple and contented life, involving church, the gym, helping me with my business, and socializing with friends. She also assisted Millie every Wednesday with her weekly grocery shopping at Sainsbury's. One day, she randomly spotted my grandad Freddie in the aisles, and she was shocked at his appearance. My grandmother, who'd done everything in the house for him, had passed away from cancer a few years prior, so he was living on his own. To hear my mum tell it, my grandad now looked like a homeless person. He used to be so meticulous about his grooming, and now he had matted hair, an unkempt beard, and his clothes were filthy.

Although Mum wasn't sure what to do, Millie urged her to go and speak to him. 'Janette,' she said, 'that is your father. I know you're hurt, but go and acknowledge him at least. I'll wait right here. You'll be fine.' Despite everything, Mum always reserved a space in her heart for the possibility of change from her family, so she left Millie and walked toward him.

Seeing her, he was overcome with emotion. 'Do you need any help, Freddie?' she asked him.

As he replied, 'Oh Janette, waaaiz, yes. Yes please,' his eyes started to well up. Here was a man who'd shown no remorse or emotion in his entire life, but he was now completely vulnerable – alone and helpless. When my mum took Freddie home, the neglect was evident, and she realized he was in dire need of assistance.

That evening, Mum shared this encounter with me, and informed me that from this point forward, she was going to take Freddie food shopping once a week. I was infuriated – remember, we'd spent most of our lives healing from his harm. I couldn't understand why she would welcome him back into our lives. I argued with her, saying, 'Why are you bringing him back into our space? I don't want him near you. He's just going to hurt to us again. If he's like this now, well, so what – that's his karma, fuck it.'

But Mum was resolute. 'Meggan,' she said, 'you have to learn when it's time to forgive, and this is what it looks like.'

Understanding the power of forgiveness

It took me about six months to gradually soften my stance. Initially, I didn't want anything to do with their revived relationship, which evolved from weekly encounters to more frequent visits. I kept my distance. But I began to see how Mum was taking all the lessons she'd learned in therapy to build a healthier relationship with her father. It was a completely different dynamic to the one from before.

I'd never seen a healthy relationship between them. He was always the abuser, and she was the victim. But this time, she implemented clear boundaries and wouldn't tolerate any misbehavior. If he behaved like an idiot, she'd say, 'Right, I'm going now; you're not going to ruin my day!' She had control over her emotions and experience of the relationship. And to my surprise, he respected her boundaries. One day I saw him at his front door, and it was like the life was back into him. He looked so rejuvenated, almost youthful. My mum's love had seemingly revived him.

Reflecting on it now, it was such a beautiful act of healing on my mum's part. To rebuild a relationship with someone who had been a source of pain from a position of self-love was remarkable. The relationship had moved from being something she depended on and was damaged by, to being something that she wanted and conducted on *her* terms. It brought her peace in her final years. The experience showed me the power of forgiveness in the most vivid way.

It showed me how forgiveness can liberate not just the person you're forgiving, but also settle the emotional turmoil inside the person that forgives.

Over time, I also rebuilt a civil relationship with my grandfather. He was unexpectedly supportive when my mum passed away. When I was stuck in Saint Lucia, with the task of transporting my mum's vessel to Trinidad, during the pandemic when the airports were closed, my grandfather helped financially, and made it possible for me to hire a small plane to bring her home. It's something I will always be thankful for.

When I got back to the UK, I looked after him as his health declined. It was my mum's request that I continue her efforts with her father if she was to pass. At the time, I reluctantly agreed, but little did I know that this duty would help aid my healing journey, too. I helped renovate his house so he could sell it before moving into a home. He's now in the early stages of dementia and doesn't recall much of the past. However, everyone in the home adores him; they say he brings joy to the home, a stark contrast to who he once was.

I'm convinced that it was my mum's act of forgiveness that sparked this transformation. My mum invested her love into him, with healthy limitations and boundaries, which made him feel loved and lightened in turn. Now all these strangers are experiencing the best version of my grandad that ever existed! And while it's ironic, I don't feel bitter.

This transformation is a testament to the power of forgiveness. One of his children forgave him, which enabled him to alter his behavior and learn to give and receive love again. Sometimes, when I look at my grandad, I see a living lesson, manifested in human form. He showed up in the end, for both my mum and me – something I never anticipated.

Why we should embrace forgiveness

This story underscores the importance of forgiveness and the value of including others in our healing process. My mum led the way in forgiving my grandad, and in time, I followed her example. It was a lengthy journey, riddled with self-doubt, but eventually we found a way to forge a new relationship with him that was healthy for the both of us.

Although everything we go through is deeply personal, and we need to work through our own shit, we do not exist as islands, completely independent of everyone else. It's easy to underestimate how much of an impact others' journeys have on us, but it's *huge*. If we think about the people in our lives who have caused us emotional harm – in whatever way that might be – it's likely that they are hurting too, and that their pain is expressed outwardly, toward others. Their journey becomes our journey when our paths cross.

I'm not implying that every wrong or every person who has hurt us warrants forgiveness. There are many, many transgressions that are unforgiveable, and sometimes others are not ready to rehabilitate themselves, or willing to confront themselves and accept what they've done. But many others are.

Rehabilitation is one of the most powerful tools we have at our disposal as humans – we have the ability to improve ourselves, to correct our mistakes, to evolve, and to express remorse. To put our hands up and say, 'Forgive me, I'm sorry' is a courageous act. When we're on our own path of healing and self-betterment, extending a hand to someone else who is on a similar journey is a profound and compassionate gesture.

How forgiveness nurtures

In choosing to reconcile with her father, my mum found a heightened sense of peace during the final years of her life. She was able to heal and nourish her own heart. Witnessing this transformation taught me the incredible strength of forgiveness. It's not an easy path, but when approached with sincerity, it becomes a replenishing source of renewal and healing.

How forgiveness protects

At first, I honestly believed I was safeguarding my mum by convincing her not to allow grandad back into her life. Yet she told me firmly, 'I've made my choice; this is what I'm doing. I would really appreciate it if you supported me in this, but I understand if you can't.' When I saw how she redefined their relationship on terms that protected her emotional well-bring, I learned a valuable lesson. Building connections on such foundations doesn't drain our energy; instead, it enhances our lives.

We release control and allow room for destiny

Control is a recurring theme in this book. It's featured in so many different aspects of my life and the lives of those around me.

I've seen relatives try to control their children, sabotaging opportunities that came their way, and destroying relationships in the process. I came to the realization that I was avoiding my own problems by attempting to 'fix' and influence the paths my friends were taking, instead of focusing on my own. I've observed many friends, as well as myself, lose ourselves to superficial distractions because our egos controlled us. And I let fear dominate me and keep me living a half-life, trapped by the prospect of failure.

In so many of these situations, these efforts at control were pointless. A waste of time and energy. My relatives' children were never going to be happy on the path their parents wanted them to follow; neither were my friends when I tried to do the same. They all had their own destinies in life and guess what – it wasn't up to me or their families to decide what that was. What's more, as you know, I was shielding myself from my own uncomfortable truths by using this sort of control as a device of distraction.

The truth is, there are aspects of life that simply lie beyond our control, whether it's about us or others. Some things are going to happen to us, regardless. These events can range from joyful surprises, like meeting the love of our life, to tragedies, like the death of someone close. When I got tested for the breast cancer BRCA gene, it took me nearly a year to read the results. Almost everyone in my family has passed away from cancer. And fortunately, I don't have it, which I'm so grateful for – but there's nothing I could've done to influence or control that outcome. And it's not just about illness, or tragedies or triumphs – I believe there is a wonderful karmic inevitability to much of our existence, and the more we try to resist it, the unhappier we'll be.

It can be a difficult concept to grasp; and this idea might seem at odds with the theme of this book, which has largely focused on confronting ourselves and reclaiming control over our lives from harmful influences. And I stand by that. But sometimes, when we abuse and overuse control, it can work against us. We can become obsessed with it as a tool and begin to believe we can control *everything* – whether that's people, situations, future outcomes, whatever. This inevitably leads to frustration and disappointment. And the areas in which I believe control can become dangerous is when it crosses over with perfectionism, avoidance, and manifesting.

How we abuse control through perfectionism...

An obsessive pursuit of perfection can wreak havoc on our mental and emotional balance. I wrote a lot about this in Part 1, so there's no need to reiterate everything here. However, it's worth reminding ourselves that attempting to control things like our appearance or presentation, in pursuit of an unattainable 'ideal,' is literally a path to unhappiness and misery. And that goes for obsessively trying to be a perfect 'better' person, too.

We can begin to release this attachment to perfectionism by appreciating the beauty of what exists right now.

Recognizing our own completeness involves embracing the abundance of our character and rejecting the notion of perfection, because it simply doesn't exist.

Nobody ever demanded perfection from us, not even the universe, which is itself a study in imperfect beauty. Breaking away from this habit isn't straightforward, but small steps can make a significant difference. Consider unfollowing people on social media who make you feel inadequate. Avoid using filters. Embrace the fact that you're flawed, we're all flawed, and we will continue to be, regardless of our efforts.

...through avoidance strategies

Another harmful way in which control reveals itself is through avoidance. As you know, I spent years escaping myself by attempting to control the lives of others, under the veil of being 'helpful.' It's something we see a lot in this life – and it might be something you're guilty of, too. If you feel that you have an unhealthy fixation with someone else's life choices, beyond what might be a normal level of involvement for a friend or family member, it's time to pause and reflect.

Question your motives: Why is this important to you? Why do you feel responsible for managing this, instead of them? Are you allowing them to follow their own path or are you trying to create it for them? Do they genuinely want this, or are you using their life as a way to sidestep your own issues? It's essential to be brutally honest with yourself.

Someone else's life isn't yours to run, no matter how noble your intentions.

...and through misunderstanding manifesting

And last, the concept of control becomes problematic when we confuse it with manifesting. Now, this is a big one. Manifestation is a term that's gained significant traction in recent years. People often talk about manifesting their dreams into reality, but there's a deeper meaning to this practice. So, what does manifesting actually mean?

True manifestation is about being patient with yourself and honoring the process. With a combination of hard work, consistency, and persistence, what's meant to be will not pass you. Just leave some room for miracles and breakthroughs to happen and let go of trying to have control over every single aspect to your life. Start small, go slow.

How allowing room for destiny nurtures

By becoming comfortable with the concept of destiny, we allow ourselves to understand that life is bigger than just us and the decisions we make. Acknowledging that we can't control everything that is intended for us is a process of gentle acceptance. Instead, we should give thanks for what we have, while aspiring for more and allowing life's journey to unfold at its natural rhythm. What we are destined to receive will arrive in due time.

How allowing room for destiny protects

Nothing happens coincidentally, nor are we in full control of the direction our path takes. When we appreciate this, we can let go of the feelings of frustration when things don't align with our schedule. We protect ourselves by taking our foot off this fast-paced life, and the delayed gratification for the good things that do come our way makes them feel all the sweeter.

True manifestation is about being patient with yourself and honoring the process. Leave some room for miracles and breakthroughs to happen and let go of trying to have control over every single aspect to your life. Start small, go slow.

We learn to let go
when it's time

Well, here we are. We've arrived at the final chapter of this book. You and I have journeyed together to this point, making it the perfect moment to delve into the topic of endings. Because if there's one thing that's inevitable in this life, it's endings.

Our lives consist of numerous, perhaps countless, individual experiences that form distinct chapters within our existence. Each of these chapters has its own beginning and, inevitably, its own conclusion.

In the process of writing this book, I've had to go through my life with meticulous attention, sifting through my memories, encounters, and experiences to find meaning and translate them into words. It's been an intense journey, but it's also showed me how naturally our lives are formed of beginnings and endings. New chapters constantly spark into life, and to evolve and grow as people, we need to say goodbye to old chapters, too.

Some of these life chapters unfold organically – they are circumstantial. Milestones like transitioning from primary to secondary school, or the journey from childhood to adulthood, and the accompanying changes that happen regardless of whether we want them to or not! And some chapters are created by dealing with the shocks that come out of nowhere, like losing our loved ones. Since losing my mum in 2021, I've experienced what feels like a second psychological death and rebirth. As I mentioned before, the first time was triggered by her initial cancer diagnosis – it forced me to take a hard look at who I'd become (an insecure ego-obsessive) and start focusing more on what was important in life.

New beginnings and old chapters

It's in the last few years that I feel I've truly begun to become the next iteration of myself – and that's a life change that I deliberately put into effect. I look back at my younger adult self now and I see someone who was still in the early stages of growth. These days, because of everything I've endured, and genuinely learning to survive the brutal knocks of life, I recognize a person who has reconstructed their life from the ground up.

I've put so much work into healing and changing my own narrative – how I saw myself, how I was harming my own heart, and how I was getting in my own way. In losing my mum – my epitome of love, my life-force, my best friend, the only person I counted as true family for my entire life – I was left utterly alone. But in the process of healing, I came to understand that I am all I have. As life progressed for those around me, I realized it was time to rebuild my own life.

Embarking on this healthier chapter in my life means I have to say goodbye and part ways with some of the old ones. So, farewell and goodbye to the person I used to be, and to the people I had to release from my life who were attached to that version of me. Some of these goodbyes are by choice, others are not.

Many endings are tough, often far from pleasant, but they're essential and unavoidable parts of our journey.

Why we struggle to accept change

It's interesting how challenging change can be, despite it being a fundamental aspect of the human experience. Nothing and nobody stays the same – yet it's one of our greatest struggles. We often want situations, people, our families, and friends to remain a constant, but change is inevitable. When change happens – as it must and will do – it can completely knock us sideways. Significant life alterations, such as the ending of a long-term relationship, or even a small shift in our current circumstances, like a new boss at work, can lead to feelings of confusion and disorientation. We might feel unsettled, and sometimes we even resist the change, through denial, anger, or by seeking – futilely – to restore the previous order of things.

It's OK to feel strange when change finds us. I believe that's a natural response to feeling the ground shift underneath us – we try to keep our feet firmly planted on it! But sometimes that deep-seated fear of change can lead us to try to avoid it, doing everything in our power to prevent it from happening. Like the many other ways we inadvertently break our own hearts, we let fear dominate and keep us in a state of uncomfortable familiarity. The idea of facing change can be frightening, but avoidance only prolongs our suffering.

New chapters constantly spark into life, and to evolve and grow as people, we need to say goodbye to old chapters, too.

Feeling the fear and doing it anyway

It takes time to teach ourselves, but we need to learn to accept the notion of change, and we can start by getting comfortable with our fears. There's no need to conquer or eliminate them completely, as experiencing fear is a natural part of being human. We can start this process by acknowledging our fear, by being honest about it and how it impacts us. There was a famous self-help book written years ago by Susan Jeffers, *Feel the Fear and Do It Anyway*, and just the title alone encapsulates this approach perfectly.

We can accept that we're afraid of change, and through that acceptance, we can begin to welcome it.

My mum firmly believed in the power of change, yet when it concerned her family, she often found it challenging to enact timely changes that could have shielded her from years of hurt. She gave too many chances and tended to delay taking action until she was left with no other choice. But once she found the courage to finally face that fear, and moved past it, she enjoyed some of the best years of her life. She closed one chapter and opened another, and during these years, she was so filled with light and vitality.

Even during her last months, she expressed to me how much she cherished her life, especially after gaining the mental freedom to distance herself from her family. While she was an incredible role model for me, she was also vocal about the importance of starting my healing journey earlier than she'd done. 'Baby, please don't wait until you're 60 before you start living a fulfilled life,' she told me.

Learning to let go along the way

We don't have to wait until we reach our final chapter of healing to start recreating our new life; changes can be implemented and enjoyed along the way. By welcoming new habits – no matter how small they might seem, like getting off the bus a stop earlier for a longer walk, or not immediately reaching for our phones in the morning – we're acknowledging our constant evolution. We're accepting our capacity to adapt, to transform, recognizing that change is always within our reach.

Therefore, when unexpected changes like job loss, bereavement, or a relationship ending occur, we're better equipped to handle them. I'm not saying that we won't feel pain or hurt from these changes – of course we will. But we can approach these situations with caution, understanding that every chapter, no matter how significant, eventually comes to an end. This acceptance is an important part of navigating life with a gentle, honest mindset.

Welcome the fear, because this is how it feels to let go. Our healing journey truly begins when we recognize that life is perpetually evolving. As one chapter ends, another will begin – so we may as well enjoy the ride.

How learning to let go nurtures

No matter how long the journey takes, never forget that you are the creator of your own sanctuary; you're the one who must nurture and care for yourself. By accepting change as a natural part of life's journey, we start to remove the blockages that contributed to us limiting ourselves.

How learning to let go protects

Your soul knows when a chapter has come to an end. By being honest with ourselves and tuning into our intuition, we can avoid causing more pain to our hearts by resisting inevitable changes. Sometimes change feels like pain, but denying it only intensifies that pain.

Reflection

I want to stress that neither this part nor the book as a whole is about sculpting a 'finished' version of ourselves. I'm not claiming that following all this advice will make you immune to mistakes. We're all beautifully flawed beings, and embracing our flaws is not just acceptance but a vital lesson in this journey. The aim is to develop self-awareness, foster self-belief, and adopt a harmonious approach to life's challenges. And bringing our learnings with us, embracing rather than discarding them, is all good progress.

Take a moment to reflect and write down your thoughts – how you are feeling about yourself after reading this book? What resonated with you? What truths hit close to home? Are there any changes you plan to make, or have you already started implementing some of them?

Conclusion

Have you ever watched the movie *8 Mile*? It's a classic, in which Eminem portrays the character of Jimmy Smith Jr., also known as B-Rabbit, in a narrative of struggle, dreams, and resilience in the world of rap music.

My mum and I adored this film. I vividly remember the first time I watched it, and what stood out to me the most was the final rap battle, where B-Rabbit has to face down the other MC, Papa Doc.

In that scene, Eminem's character gets on stage and lays bare his entire life, his vulnerabilities, his rough background, the fact he's classed as 'white trash,' his hard life, everything. He stands, unapologetically owning his truth. When he hands the mic back to Papa Doc, his opponent is speechless. B-Rabbit has already revealed everything, leaving no ammunition for Papa Doc to use. Everyone starts booing and, no joke, it felt like the most profound thing I'd ever seen.

This approach has since become something I've implemented in my life. Because it's so hard – almost impossible, really – to bring down someone who is fully honest about themselves, embracing their flaws and all.

How we welcome in strength through honesty

The movie 8 Mile taught me a life-changing lesson: Standing in your truth without shame enables you to be indestructible. It disarms your enemies, as they have nothing to use against you. Any criticism they might have, you've already acknowledged. Moreover, it also leaves you with nothing to berate yourself about, too. No hidden truths, no secret shames. This connects to what I mentioned at the beginning of this book about the power of vulnerability. By opening ourselves up to complete honesty and shedding the facades we present to ourselves and others, we let in the possibility of truth, honesty, and strength.

Throughout this book, I've endeavored to maintain this honesty. I've been open about my failures, my darkest moments, and my journey of rebuilding through often challenging and painful transparency.

In the last few years, what kept running through my mind was this thought: *If I can do this, if I can heal from all of this, then so can others.*

It's why I'm so passionate about reinforcing the idea that life can be rebuilt, after loss, after trauma, after convincing ourselves that we aren't worthy of fully experiencing it, even if we've strayed light-years away from where we're meant to be. We *still* have the capability of returning home to ourselves and living a more fulfilled and happier existence.

Your experience of this journey

Now, I'm curious about how you're feeling after reading this book. If you've got here after reading the whole book (and not just sneaking a look at the ending, hoping to find a simple solution to life's complexities – no judgment here!), then first, *thank you.* Second, *woah, how are you doing?*

We've gone through a lot, because this book is a recollection and distillation of everything I've learned – watching my mum heal from her childhood trauma, the destructive habits I developed, and healthier ones I learned over time from my own healing journey, along with essential teachings from therapy and the wisdom obtained from the elders in the community that raised me.

We've delved deeply into how we break our own hearts, how we embark on the path to healing, and how we can sustain that healing process by nurturing and safeguarding our hearts. It's been a substantial journey, and even if it's been challenging at times, I sincerely hope it's been beneficial for you. Because that's the purpose of this book. That's why I've been so transparent in every chapter. Because by sharing our stories, we normalize our experiences and in turn, uplift one another.

Why this isn't the end

As I mentioned before, this isn't supposed to be the 'end' of our journey, just because we've opened ourselves up to honesty and vulnerability.

Our journey with healing has no expiration date. It's a natural, constant process in life: We endure, we hurt, and we heal.

Life will always throw challenges and obstacles in our way, and it's not about shutting ourselves away from future pain; it's about having the emotional tools and self-awareness to best deal with those trials. Look, you might reach a stage where all the necessary changes have been made and your new life aligns perfectly with your vision. But even as we continue to grow, we'll inevitably make new mistakes and face different challenges, which will foster further growth and learning.

What I'm trying to convey is that in this journey, there's no losing. This whole process is a win-win for everyone – not just for ourselves, but also for the people in our lives. I understand how daunting it can seem. It was for me! Almost *beyond* scary – so much so that it took me years to confront it. But the hopes of a brighter future, where the possibility of waking up free from the weight of my heavy heart was something that could *actually* happen, gave me the motivation I needed to start. It encouraged me to unearth and confront all the things I had buried deep in my past.

Reaching out for further help

I think it's important for me to highlight another crucial element in my recovery, alongside my strong determination to overcome the destructive mindset that was gradually undermining my life: the realization that I couldn't do this alone. After a lifetime of watching Mum normalize going to therapy, I was reminded by the memory of the powerful role it played in maintaining the serenity in my household.

I knew that it was the path I needed to take to realign with myself and come to terms with the depths of what I was facing and how much trauma I actively had to heal. Boy, did it open my eyes!

Beforehand, my life was in disarray. I even changed the white walls of my mum's apartment to a dark, gloomy brown, reflecting my inner turmoil. My friends were deeply concerned, thinking I was losing my mind, which I was. Consumed by sadness, I was torn between not wanting to live and yet holding onto dreams my mum had always believed I could achieve. The turning point came when my partner, who I'd just started dating, deep-cleaned my entire house while I slept. Waking up to that change was a stark realization of how much I had let myself go. As the saying goes, the state of your home is a reflection of your mind.

Recognizing when you've hit rock bottom, and when to seek professional help, is crucial. I ignored my therapist for almost a year, until my mental state became unbearable, resulting in me trembling from the PTSD and having daily panic attacks; I knew I had to reach out. The support I received over the next year was pivotal; his support saved my life. Literally. Looking back, the fragile state of my mind seems almost unimaginable now. I'm so proud of myself for recognizing my need for help, and it's something I strongly advocate for others to pursue too.

The quicker you get your resolve, the faster you can regain control of your life. Our mental health is delicate, and if something feels off, knowing when to surrender and seek help is vital. Therapy is so normalized in our generation. I mean, who *hasn't* got a therapist these days?

Seeking help isn't accepting defeat; you're simply acknowledging that you've taken yourself this far, but in order to get over this pain, you accept that you need stronger arms to hold you, until you gain the strength to hold yourself.

Through these experiences, I arrived at so many revelations, particularly one that has become the cornerstone of this book. I found it hard initially to come to terms with the fact that heartbreak isn't always the result of someone else's actions, but instead, of our own inability to handle ourselves with care. We play a significant role in creating our own pain. Once I decided to treat myself with more compassion, life opened up in so many incredible ways, and I hope – no, I *know* – it will do the same for you.

Bringing us all together with The Good Quote

I hope The Good Quote continues to be a beacon of human connection in the daily lives of all who use it. It might be a small moment, just a few seconds of reading and glancing at our phones, but these few seconds can have an enormous impact. The right words put together in the right way can unite us all together in the common thread of humanity. There's an intention behind each upload that impacts our readers in ways that stretch far beyond our interpretation. We plant seeds of hope into the hearts of millions daily, and despite not knowing where these words will land, these seeds have the potential to bloom in someone's life. Our responsibility is to simply keep planting.

Thank you again for reading this book and aligning your journey with mine. Like I said at the start, our hearts all share a mutual coherence. We all experience the same feelings and thoughts, both beautiful and brutal. We all seek connection and love. Good luck on your own journey of healing – remember that beauty resides in the journey, and **better days are waiting for us all**.

Meggan x

We endure.
We hurt.
We heal.

Acknowledgments

To the Honorable Evelyn Lobyn, the great-grandmother I never met, but felt: My whole life I heard stories about you. Mum loved and raised me, the same way you loved and raised her. Thank you for your endless sacrifices and intentional measures you put into place to raise Mum, which I too benefited from. Sleep well.

To Olive Lewis, my great-aunt: How can one woman exude so much love? When I grow up I want to be loved, just like you. The heart of our family. Memories of us all, liming on the veranda, chatting away as the sun sets. I will miss you forever. Sleep well.

To Merlin Zephyrine, my great-uncle: Thank you for your ability to bring light and ease to any situation, for reminding me to appreciate the simplicities of life, and for invoking my love for View-Points. Sleep well.

To Baba Zephyrine, my great-uncle: Serious about little, but family was where you drew the line. I'll always commend you for your efforts to be close by, if ever needed. You were the funniest man I knew. Sleep well.

To Shirley Zephyrine, my great-aunt: You lived life with intention, and always stayed true to your word and close to your Bible. The softest heart with the warmest embrace. I miss you. Sleep well.

To Pastor Williams: Thank you for always reminding me to involve God in all that I do and to reference scriptures in the Bible when calling unto God. I'm still not comfortable with praying out loud but I'm getting there. Sleep Well.

To Sammy, my godfather: A mouth full of gold and a heart full of soul. You were an honorable, credible, loyal man and I will always be grateful for the examples you set. Thanking you for being such a good friend to Mum. Sleep well.

To Tom Glaser: I remember when you were publishing your book, and how you emphasized the importance of sharing your story. Mum was up for weeks proofreading. Not only did you inspire me to work for myself, but I'm an author now too. Sleep well.

To my aunt Wilma Lewis (Welma): Thank you for checking in since Mum transitioned. I appreciate you x

To Auntie Carol and family: I love you all.

To my family in Trinidad, the Harewoods and the Zephyrines, who actively played a positive role in my childhood: Thank you for the beautiful memories and planting roots.

To Auntie Mel, Lauren, and Frankie: We reconnected just in time. I love you all.

To Millie Scarlet, my eldest friend, and the grandmother I never had: Where would I be without your prayers? Every evening, since I could remember, around 10 p.m. you would call Mum to say goodnight and pray together. You mean the world to me. Thank you for your endless wisdom, and for reminding me that there's nothing new under the sun. I love you.

To Carol Brooks, my godmother: Thank you for making Mum feel seen, heard, considered, and loved. You're the sister she never had. What a beautiful bond. Thank you for being an exceptional friend. I love you.

To Audrey Brothers, my mum's longest friend: My whole life, I watched you extend love through the kindest acts of community and support. Continue to give yourself grace. You're doing just fine. I love you.

To Lincoln Beckford and Enid Saunders: You are both kindness personified. Enid, thank you for your support and the efforts you've made over the years for our community. Lincoln, the youth program you orchestrated in the 2005 half-term has fostered friendships that have endured for over two decades. I'm grateful to you for connecting me with what I now consider my chosen family, the friends who have become an integral part of my life.

To Frank and Diana Solomon: Thank you for continuously broadening my horizons, praying over my life, pouring into me, supporting me through it all, and reminding me to always dream big. Psalms 91.

To Pastor William and Yvonne William: Thank you for creating such a beautiful church and community, and giving Mum somewhere safe to worship. Thank you for your support and for constantly checking in.

To Alan Roberts: You always had my best interests at heart. Business advice, endless support, and tough love. I wish I'd listened to you sooner. Good thing I still have room to grow.

To Jermaine and Rochelle: Against all odds, we turned out alright, didn't we? Lol.

To my girls: Ketema, Bianca, Raythe, Muna, and Gee. Thank you for doing life with me. I hope we all grow old together. Love always.

To Chanelle and Kingsley: Thank you for all the years of support, encouragement, opportunities, advice, introductions, and most importantly, friendship. Love.

To Malanda J.C., Rachel Wolchin, Sonya Teclai, Qiya, and Dulce Ruby: infinite, infinite love.

To Krippy & J.: 'A tree takes time to grow.'

To Jamala Osman: You taught me to be true to myself, which in turn opened up a whole new world for me. Thank you always. Don't ever stop pouring into yourself.

To Hussain Manawer: I genuinely believe that nobody works harder than you. You inspire me more than words can express. The Original Mummy's Boy is changing the world, one step at a time.

To Tomi Olarewaju: I will always believe you were sent from God, and anything gifted from God, I vow to honor and cherish for life. I'll always be here for you. Thank you for reminding me what it feels like to be genuinely loved, seen, heard, and appreciated.

To Michael and Steve: Divine alignment connected us. I wouldn't be here without your support. Thank you for pouring into me and getting me back on my feet. I wish you were both able to meet Mum. I'm blessed and honored to have you both in my life. Thank you.

To my agent, Tim Moore: I remember walking down Baker Street, envisioning this exact moment. Your dedication to turning this dream into reality has been exceptional. You are indeed the agent that every writer dreams of having by their side.

To Wale Kalejaiye: A decade of nurturing dreams and watching them grow. It's been an incredible journey of depth and transformation. You knew I needed to do this, to finally take the step, and be bold enough to share this story. Thank you for your patience and support, and for being a source of strength, particularly in moments when I was still piecing it all together. I admire your spirit of tenacity and I pray you continue to flourish in all that you pour yourself into. Thank you for being the foundation of this journey, for making every possibility we imagined come true. Thank you for being my friend.

To Becky and Vimbai: Thank you both for being an integral part of this journey. Thank you for your dedication and expertise, transforming the essence of this book into something truly magical.

To my commissioning editor Kezia Bayard-White: I believe that synergy was the foundation of our collaboration. From the initial steps of this journey to every moment that followed, you fostered a nurturing space that allowed me to immerse myself fully in this project. Thank you for your encouragement, our meet-ups at the coffee shop, your unwavering firmness during the days when things got too heavy, and for continually challenging me to push myself beyond my limits. Your dedication is a testament to the spirit of Hay House, and I sincerely thank you for everything.

To the entire team at Hay House: Thank you for offering a warm and welcoming space for my story to take root. Being a part of the Hay House family, where my journey has been embraced and supported, is an honor that fills my heart with gratitude.

About the Author

Meggan Roxanne is a first-generation British-Trinidadian author, entrepreneur, digital artist, speaker, and the inspirational force behind the renowned platform The Good Quote (**@thegoodquote**).

After dropping out of university, working a job that was draining her energy and spirit, and battling with anxiety and depression, Meggan launched a Tumblr blog that became an overnight sensation. From this, Meggan's company, The Good Co, was born – a positive platform that creates and publishes original content through social media, videos, articles, and podcasts to encourage motivation, positive thinking, higher-vibrational living, and well-being.

Meggan has built a community of over 30 million people dedicated to mental health awareness, wellness, and self-development.

HAY HOUSE

CONNECT WITH

HAY HOUSE
ONLINE

🌐 hayhouse.co.uk   **f** @hayhouse

📷 @hayhouseuk   𝕏 @hayhouseuk

▶ @hayhouseuk   ♪ @hayhouseuk

Find out all about our latest books & card decks • Be the first to know about exclusive discounts • Interact with our authors in live broadcasts • Celebrate the cycle of the seasons with us • Watch free videos from your favourite authors • Connect with like-minded souls

'The gateways to wisdom and knowledge
are always open.'

Louise Hay